MILFORD ZORNES

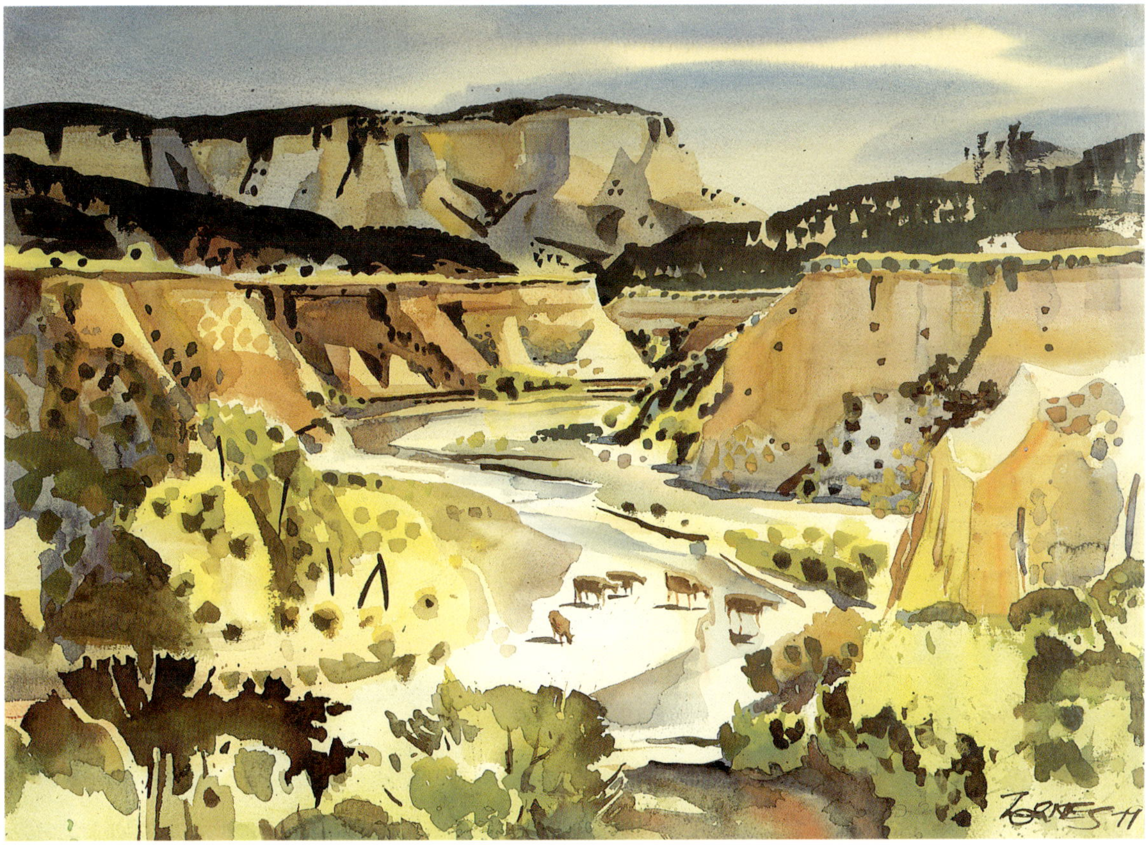

Deer Creek Crossing. Watercolor 22 x 30 in. Dr. and Mrs. Neerhout Collection.

for [illegible]
Milford Zornes A.N.A
12/18/91

BY GORDON T. McCLELLAND and MILFORD ZORNES

HP

Hillcrest Press, Inc.
P.O. Box 10636
Beverly Hills, CA 90210

ISBN 0-914589-07-5

Edited by Jay T. Last and Zena Pearlstone
Designed by Gordon T. McClelland
Graphic Production by Birgitta Thornton
Photography by Mike Rupp

Printed and bound in Japan by Dai Nippon
Typography by Consolidated Resources, Fountain Valley, California

ACKNOWLEDGEMENTS: GORDON T. McCLELLAND

A very special thanks to Jay T. Last for encouragement and the many hours spent talking over and working out ideas for this project. Most of the biographical information in this book came from a series of interviews I conducted with Milford Zornes between 1983 and 1991 and from information found in his scrap books, exhibition catalogs and files. Additional assistance in locating paintings and information came from Barbara Beretich, Gary Breitweiser, Gerald Buck, Orville Clarke Jr., Janet Dominik, Betty Davenport Ford, Robert George, David Hoy, Glen and Pam Knowles, Mike Rupp, Clyde Singer, George Stern, Mike and Susan Verbal, John and Nancy Weare, Greg Young and Pat Zornes. The private collectors and institutions that allowed us to photograph and reproduce works from their collections are credited in the caption under their picture. My sincere thanks to all of these people for their help in making this book possible.

ACKNOWLEDGEMENTS: MILFORD ZORNES

I'd like to dedicate my efforts on this book project to my wife Patricia. Thanks to Betty Davenport Ford, Rex Brandt, Tony Couch, Naomi Brotherton, Judy Betts, Gerald Brommer, Virginia Tognazzini, Dr. Richard H. Hancock, James and Celest Baker, Sheila Parsons, Loanne Paul King, Bernice Hutchison, Marjorie Harvey, Tom Wood, Stan Kania and Gilbert Garcia, for sharing encouragement through my career and the production of this book. Also, I'd like to share this quote from William Blake: "To the eyes of the man of imagination, nature is imgination itself."

Table of Contents

1

1908–1942

"If an artist is honest to the influences which have shaped his work and honest in his interpretation of nature and his design concepts, personal style will emerge."

—M.Z.

Milford Zornes was born on his grandfather's farm in western Oklahoma on January 25, 1908. His father, James Francis, was a farmer and rancher, his mother Clara, a school teacher. Virginia, his sister, was born in 1911.

Most of Zornes' early childhood was spent on the windswept prairie near Camargo, where his father and relatives labored at farming and cattle raising under adverse conditions. Often they suffered hot dusty summers and bitter cold winters but all of this was tempered by fond memories of special events. Zornes recalled: "There were the exciting experiences of harvest time when many men of the community shared work and great numbers came to the bountiful tables of food that the women prepared. We were involved in cattle drives, experienced the changing seasons and had close contact with the land. We raised animals and played in the hot sun; things and conditions that caught my youthful imagination."

The local one-room school houses offered short, irregular terms because of low funds and the need to allow the children to work on farms when help was needed. Bad weather and poor road conditions also made it difficult for many to attend school. This erratic schooling was a concern to Zornes' parents so they arranged for him and his sister to live part time in town, where they could have the advantage of a better educational system.

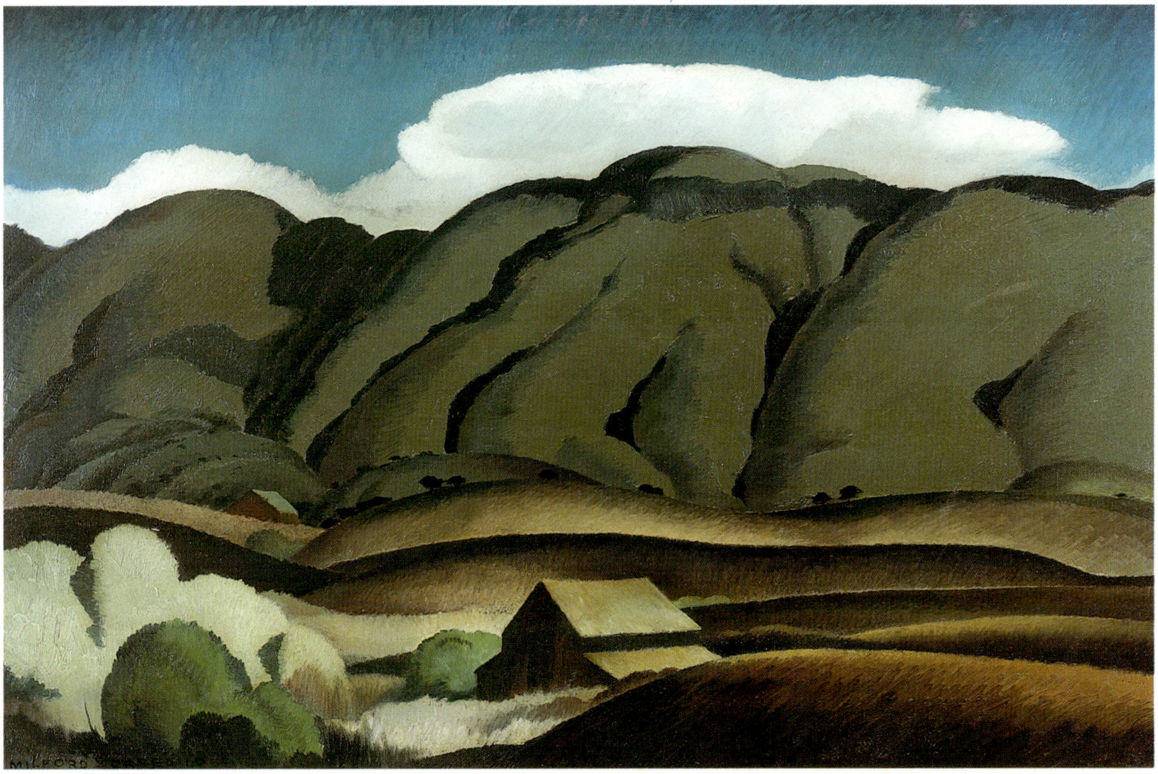

Nipomo Hills. 1936 Oil on Canvas 24 x 26 in. Collection of Joseph Moure.

Although Zornes' father was not a well educated person, he encouraged his son and set a good example. Zornes stated: "My father's ethic was a simple one of honesty and hard work. He had imagination and ideas that always have been and still are my surest guide."

In 1922 the family moved to Boise, Idaho where Zornes attended public school. He reluctantly took violin lessons to please his father, but his heart was in drawing. Although he had no training other than brief instruction from his mother, Zornes became "the kid who could draw." His talent bloomed in the high school annual and often he produced pictures for friends and relatives. Occasionally he would receive small amounts of money for drawing pictures of pets or children.

During his junior year of high school Zornes sustained an injury to his left eye while playing football, forcing him to drop out of school for a semester. This release from school led to his first adventure away from home. Since he was tall for his seventeen years he said he was nineteen and thus became eligible to he hired by the United States General Land Office Survey Service as a lineman on a survey crew.

There were six men on the crew and together they traveled across Idaho on mule-drawn wagons, sectioning townships near the lava flows of Minadoka County. By summer they reached the west boundry of Yellowstone National Park, a region that had not previously been surveyed or mapped. While traveling they lived in large tents. Their only contact with

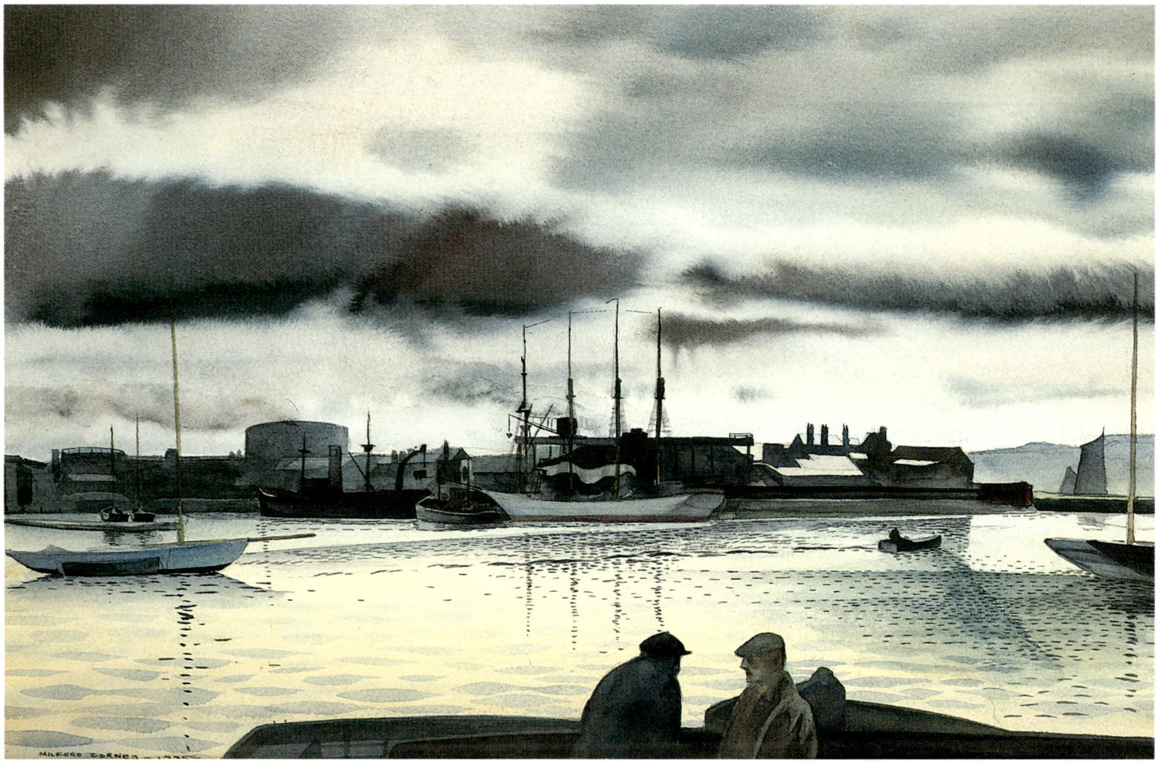

The Coal Jetty. 1935 Watercolor 15 x 21 in. The Butler Institute of American Art.

the outside world was through the packer who took mules down to the Snake River Valley and then drove a truck to Ashton to pick up mail and supplies. The cook was an old cowboy, a true product of the pioneer west. He spun tales of adventure and taught the young men to shoot, fish and know the woods. Zornes enjoyed this period and wrote prolifically of his experiences to his parents and sister.

After this season of adventure and work Zornes traveled to California to join his family. They had moved to the San Fernando Valley where his father became involved in the building industry. At this time Southern California was experiencing a major land boom and a dramatic increase in population. Suburban cities around Los Angeles were rapidly growing as the motion picture industry flourished, oil was discovered and the Pacific Electric public transportation system made commuting a possibility.

Of this time Zornes recalled: ''We lived near the San Fernando Mission and I was intrigued by the buildings and grounds when we first moved to the area. They seemed to epitomize the romantic impressions I had from reading stories about California and the Spanish explorers' and padres' influence on this part of the country. Throughout the entire region there were seemingly endless rows of orange trees and towering snow capped mountains. I saw the Pacific Ocean for the first time, it was all very exciting.''

In the fall of 1926 Zornes graduated from San Fernando High School and began thinking about a career that would pay as well as provide travel

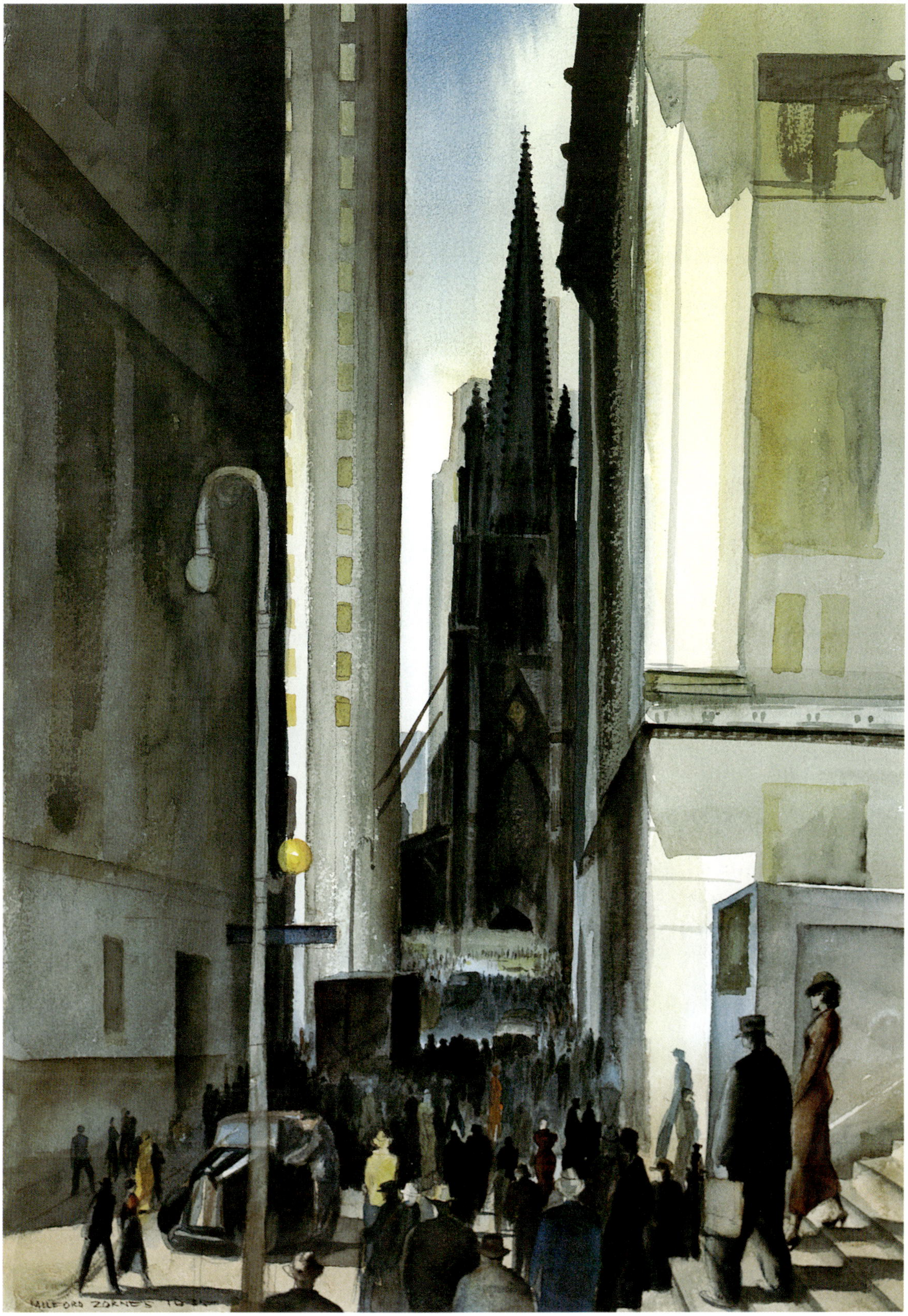

The Canyon. 1935 Watercolor 22 x 15 in. Private Collection.

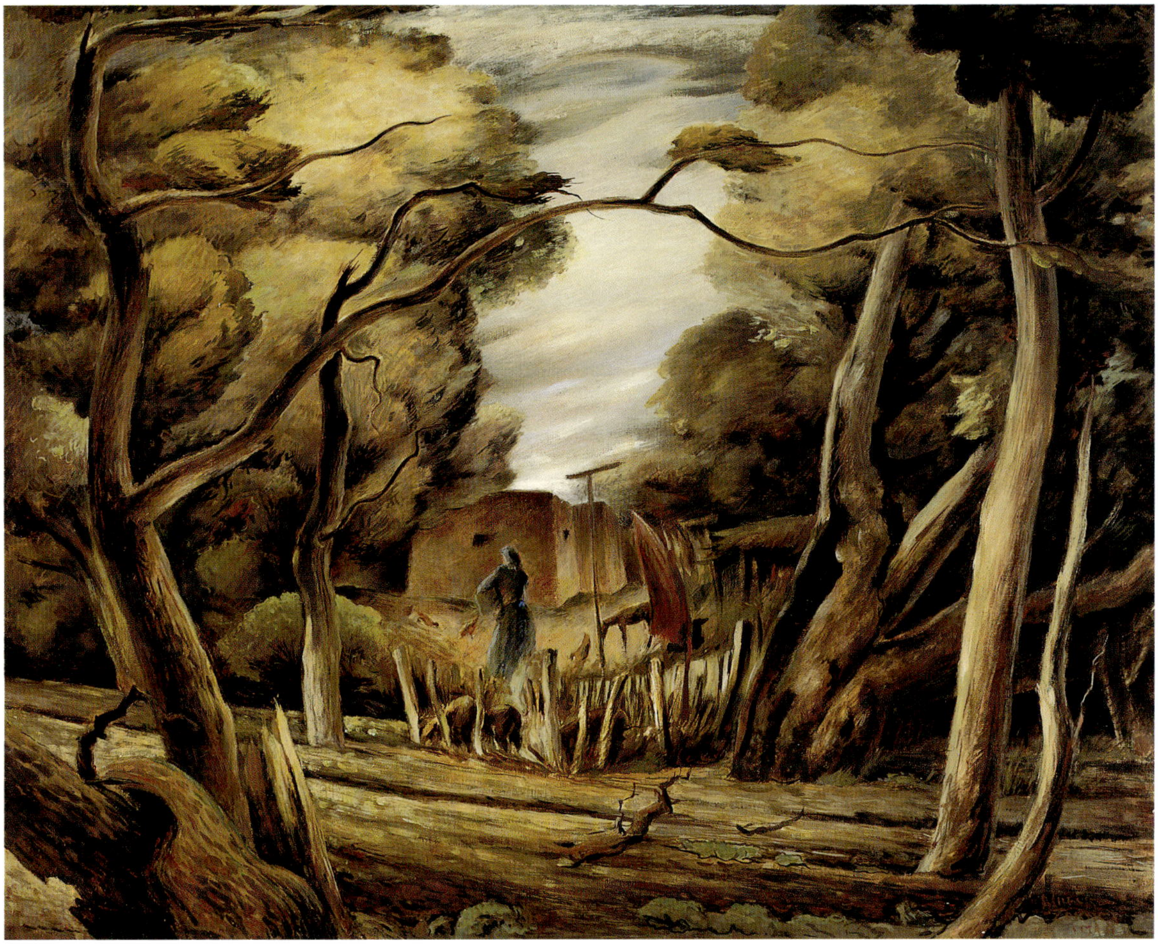

At Maricopa. 1940 Oil on Canvas 29 x 35 in. John and Nancy Weare Collection.

and adventure. His first idea was to become a freelance newsreel cameraman and reporter. He purchased a used Pathe motion picture camera and set out to cover local events. Although he soon realized that this was not the career he wanted, some of his assignments did provide excitement. In one case he traveled to Nevada to cover a potential gold strike; in actuality, a hoax by some movie personalities to bring life to the old ghost town of Goldfield in which they had real estate business investments. While the "big story" never materialized, the trip gave him the opportunity to visit another part of the southwest.

Shortly after this adventure he moved to Santa Maria, a small town on the central coast of California and attended junior college from 1927 to 1928. During this time he worked as a freelance writer and had several stories published in *Popular Mechanics* and *Scientific American*. He then studied, for a short time, at Hearld's Engineering School in San Francisco where he explored the idea of becoming an architect.

Not being able to settle on a career, Zornes hitchhiked to San Diego, across the southern states and then north to New York City. In New York he worked on the docks while waiting to ship out in the Merchant Marines. After several months he signed on to a Moore-McCormick Line freighter, bound for Denmark.

When the freighter docked in Copenhagen, Zornes jumped ship and began traveling across Europe, walking, hitchhiking and bicycling. This first European trip was in many ways a dream come true. Zornes wrote: "It was springtime in Denmark. Beech forests were coming out into new leaf. Everything was neat and clean in the countryside. Cattle in green pastures were tethered so that they grazed evenly. Farm yards were beautifully laid out, firewood stacked in tiers, farmers in top hats and tails driving their families to church in carriages. It was a story book land under the blue northern skies."

From Denmark he traveled across Germany, Luxemburg and into France. In Paris he viewed art treasures in the Louvre, visited the Left Bank and experienced whatever he could with his limited funds. When finally out of money, he went to Le Havre and boarded a ship bound for New York. On the return voyage Zornes began thinking about the art he viewed in European museums and decided to visit some American museums upon his arrival on the East Coast.

For several months Zornes thumbed his way around, visiting museums in New York, Philadelphia and Baltimore. He then signed on as an engine-room worker on a freighter headed to San Pedro via the Panama Canal. Zornes arrived in California just as the stock market crash of 1929 was beginning to effect the West Coast economy.

For many this was a difficult time of adjustment, but for Zornes it did not make much difference. He commented: "During those years I was so monetarily poor anyway that the Great Depression seemed somewhat business as usual to me! I was a young man and had no real responsibility except to give thought to the plaguing problem of what to do."

In 1930 Zornes attended several art exhibitions in Southern California and made a definite decision to study art. He enrolled at the Otis Art Institute in Los Angeles and received additional instruction from F. Tolles Chamberlin in Pasadena. The following year Zornes was awarded a scholarship to attend Pomona College in Claremont.

About this time Zornes also saw a one-man show of art works by Millard Sheets. He recalled: "When I first became aware of Millard, I was impressed by the fact that this young man, only a year older than me, was already making a name for himself in the art world. He was from a local family, had grown up in the Pomona Valley where I lived and was painting pictures of the Chino hills and other scenes that I looked at every day.

When Sheets came to teach at Scripps College, a neighboring campus to Pomona College, I was anxious to study with him, but Scripps was an all womens college. Tom Craig, another art student at Pomona and I forced the issue and were given the right to study with Sheets as well. It was clear he was able to comprehend concepts about art much more readily than Tom and myself, so the three of us spent many hours together that were most meaningful to me. In later years Millard and I had differences, but to his enthusiasm for art and his teaching and his great influence in

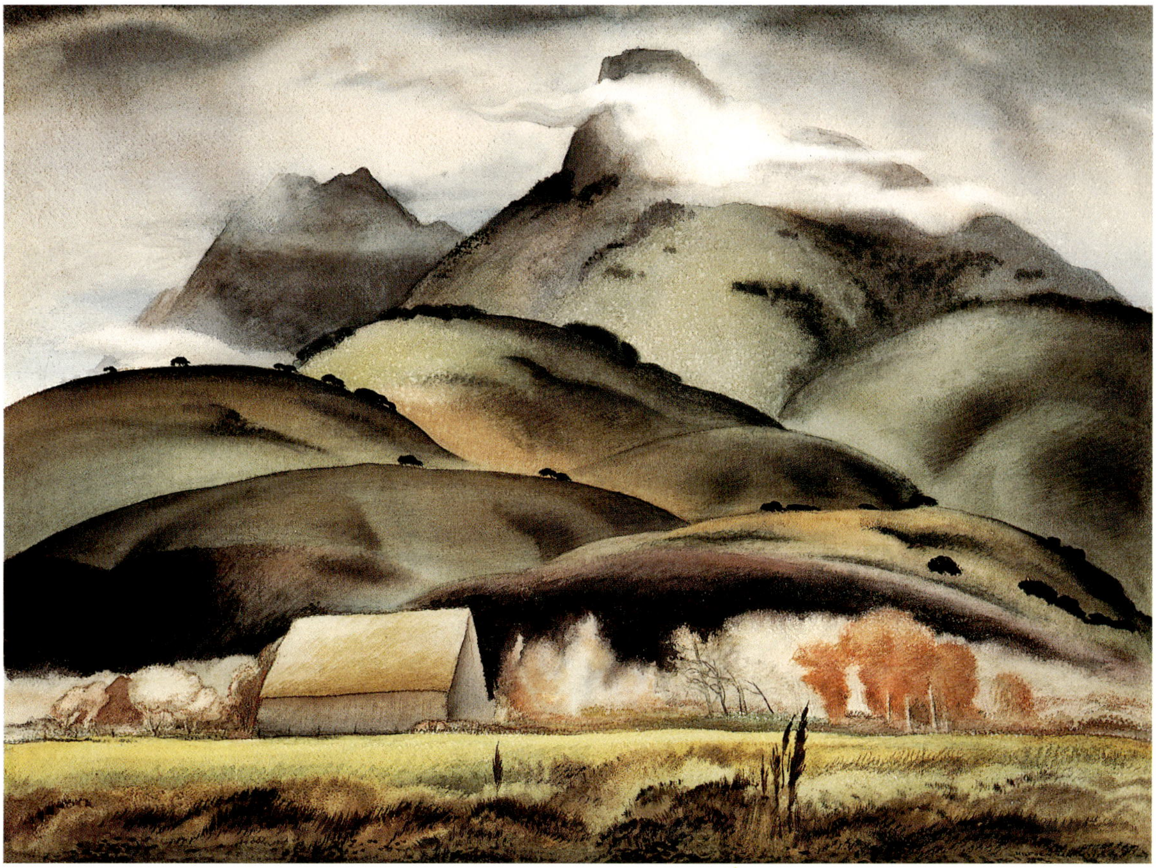

Cerro Romualdo. 1937 Watercolor 22 x 30 in. Salley and David Martin Collection.

the growth of painting in Southern California, I pay tribute with deep thanks."

Zornes and Craig became fast friends as they both vigorously pursued art careers in addition to their general college studies. Eventually they shared a small studio off campus. Zornes writes: "Tom was a big, burly, outgoing fellow and a brilliant science student in botany. He was from a family of doctors, all well educated and mentally alert. It was a stimulating association for me with my unguided background and I probably aided Tom through my willingness to go anywhere that offered excitment and new subject matter for painting."

For several years Zornes and Craig spent much of their time painting together and sharing ideas. At first they hitchhiked and hopped trains to painting sites in Northern and Central California. Later Zornes purchased an ancient Studebaker. They would fill the car with art supplies and go off on painting expeditions, determined not to come back until they painted on every canvas and sheet of paper. It was during this period that both artists made great improvements in their ability to paint, particularly in the watercolor medium.

While a student Zornes exhibited at art shows throughout the Southland and by the time he graduated was a member of the California Water Color

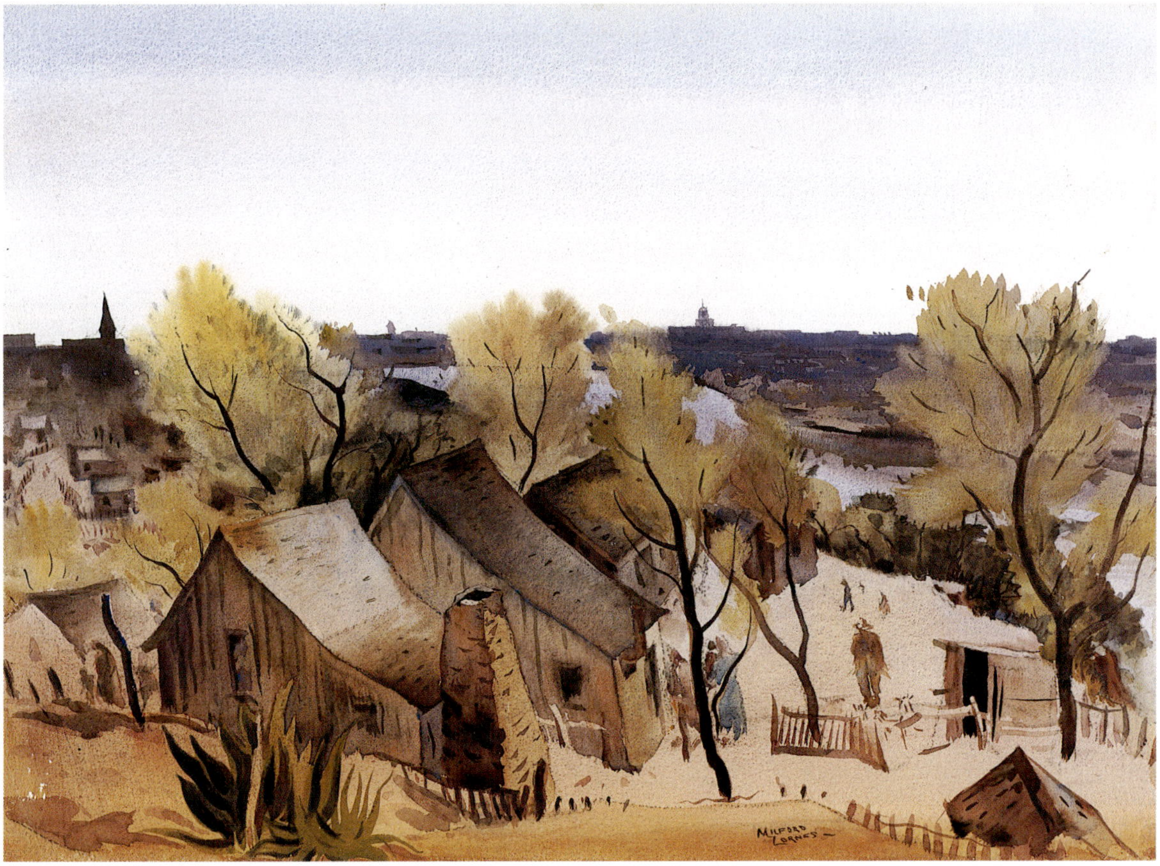

Eagle Pass. 1939 Watercolor 22 x 30 in. Mike and Susan Verbal Collection.

Society. Phil Dike, Millard Sheets, Emil Kosa Jr., Barse Miller, Paul Sample, Lee Blair, Hardie Gramatky and many other outstanding artists were also members. As a group they were receiving national acclaim for their innovative approaches to watercolor painting. All of these artists were friends or acquaintances of Zornes and together they made up the core of what was considered California's premier regional school of art from the 1930s and early 1940s.

In the spring of 1934 Zornes began producing art for the P.W.A.P., a government funded art project. On a full time basis he would go out on location and paint watercolors of landscapes and cityscapes. When these paintings were delivered to the government regional office he would receive a check. Most of these paintings were hung in public places like schools, hospitals, post offices and other government buildings. After just three months on this project Zornes began receiving attention. First his works were selected for a major exhibition of American art in the Corcoran Galleries in Washington D.C., then President and Mrs. Roosevelt chose one titled "The Old Adobe" to hang in the White House. As a result there was immediate national interest in his art work.

Following the publicity of the Roosevelt's selection, Zornes' art career accelerated. He routinely received invitations to exhibit at major museums

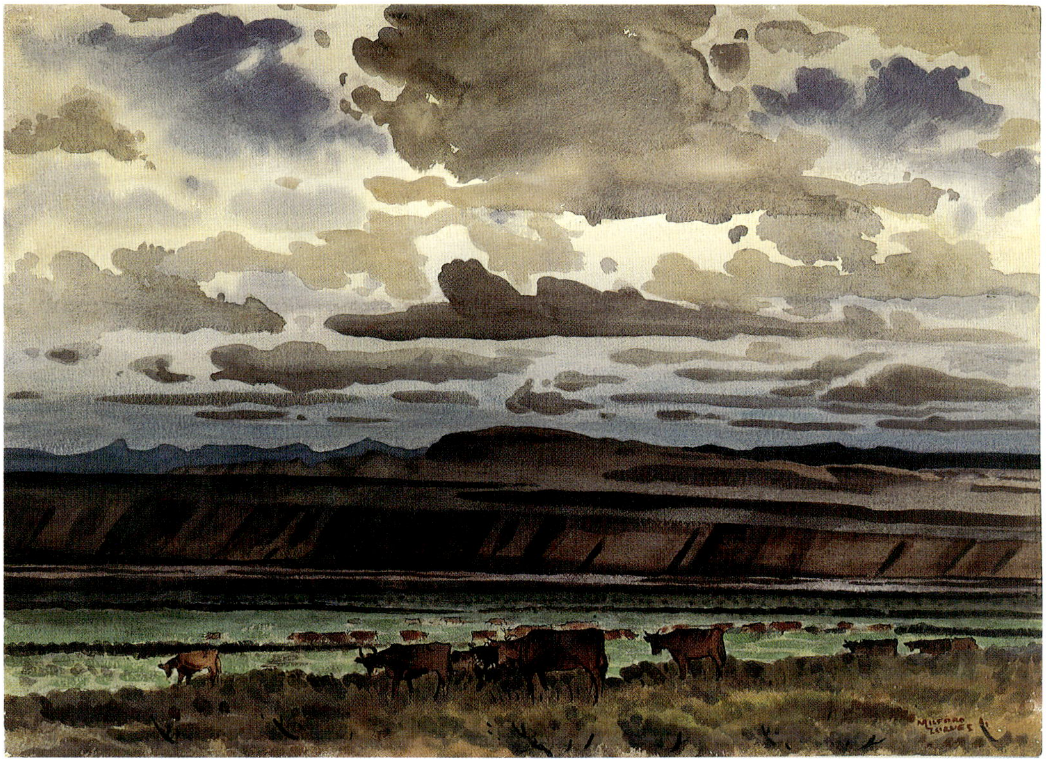

Nevada. 1941 Watercolor 22 x 30 in. Mike and Susan Verbal Collection.

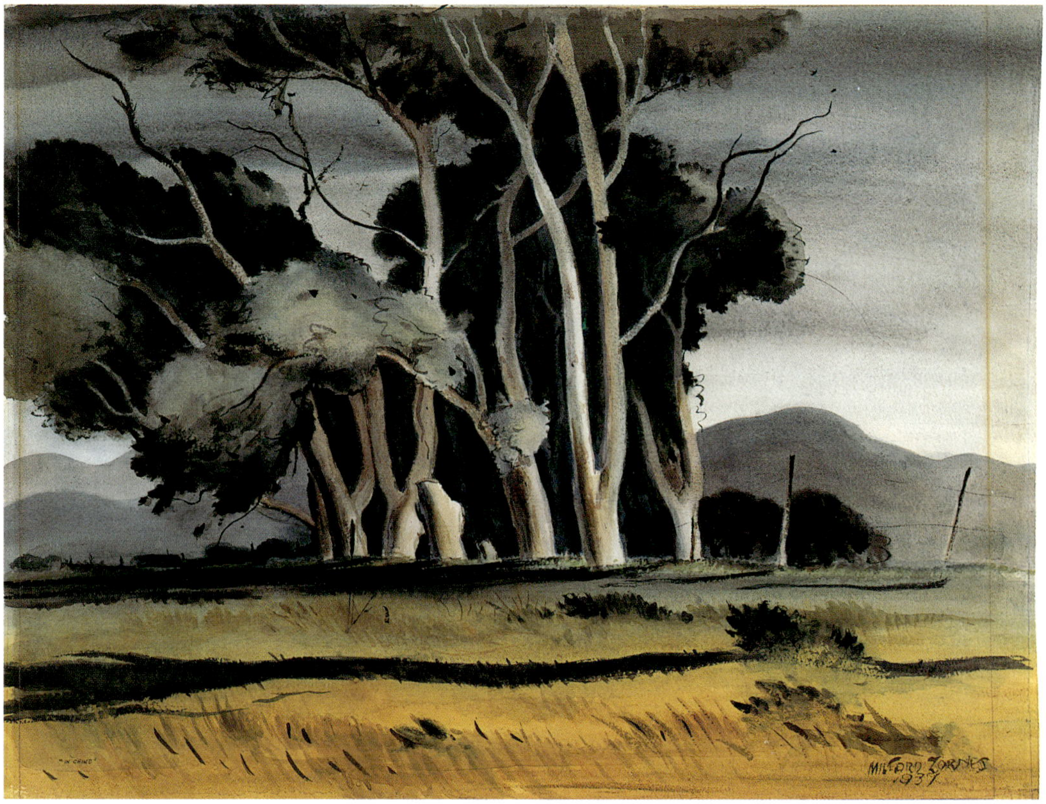

Trees in Chino. Watercolor 22 x 30 in. Mike and Susan Verbal Collection.

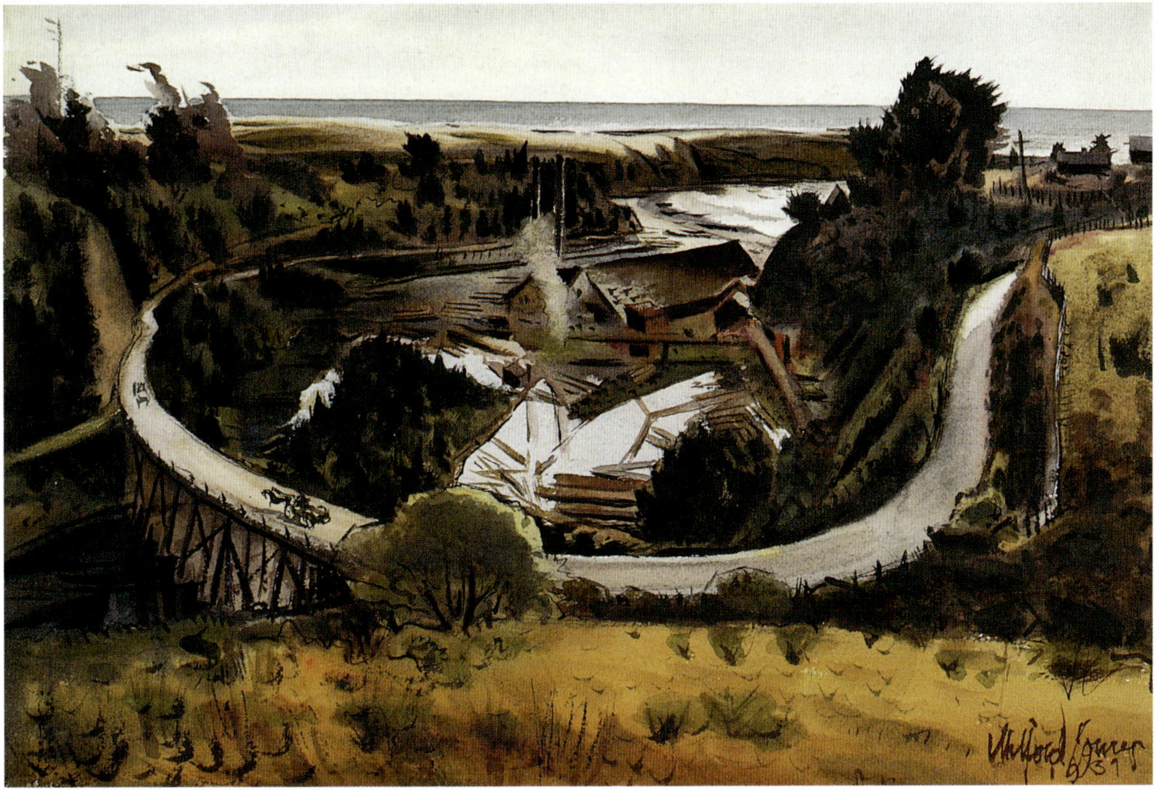

Saw Mill by the Sea. 1939 Watercolor 15 x 22 in.

throughout the country. The Metropolitan Museum of Art in New York City, Butler Art Institute in Ohio, Los Angeles County Museum of Art, San Diego Fine Arts Gallery and other prominent institutions acquired paintings by Zornes for their permanent collections. On the East Coast he was represented by the Walker Galleries in New York City and in Los Angeles by the Stendal Galleries.

In 1935 Zornes married Gloria Codd. In the early years of this marriage the couple had a home in Claremont near a small art gallery that Gloria operated. In 1936 they traveled to the East Coast and then sailed to England. Upon their return to California they met Carl Troedsson, a Swedish architect, and arranged for him to design a home constructed of glass, redwood, fieldstone, brick and corregated iron to be built at Tenth and Oxford Street in Claremont. Many local residents in this architecturally conservative neighborhood were unhappy about this ''modern'' structure which was aesthetically and functionally ahead of its time and was featured in *California Arts and Architecture* magazine. The Zornes lived in this home for the duration of the marriage (until 1940), then sold it. From this marriage came their son Franz Milford Zornes.

During this period Zornes signed up for government sponsored art projects whenever they were available. On several occasions he received let-

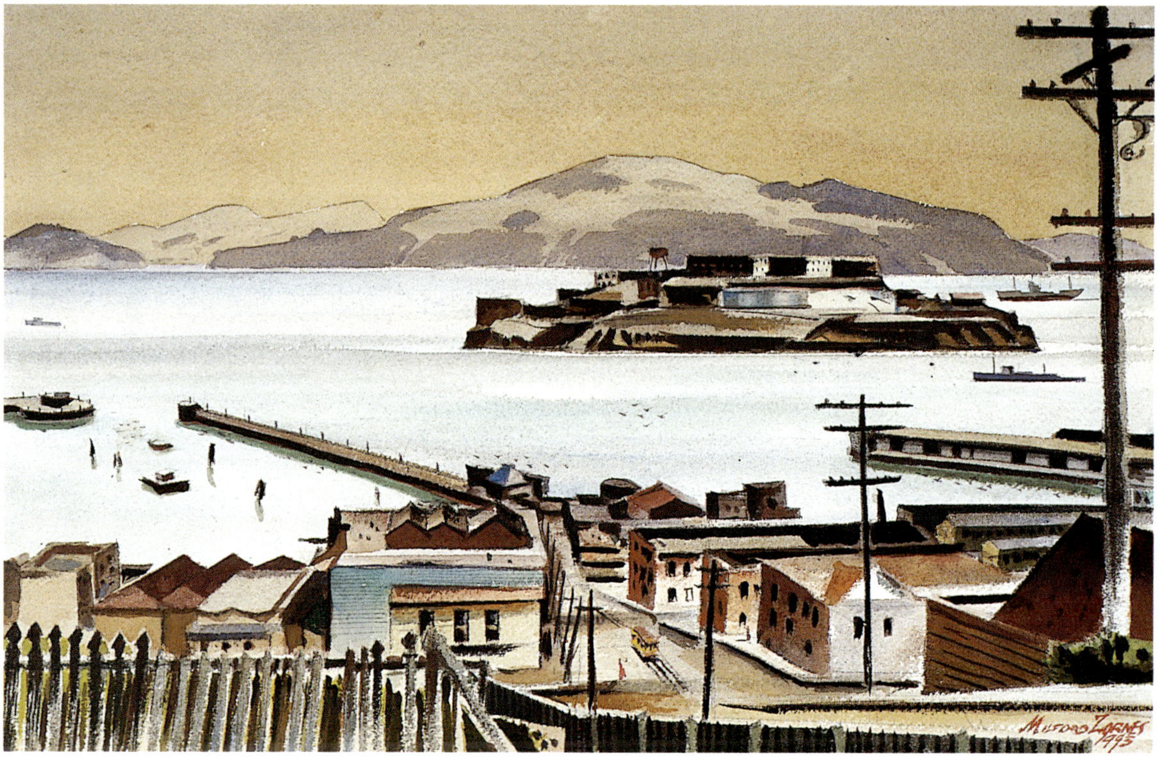

Alcatraz. 1943 Watercolor 15 x 22 in.

ters from the project headquarters, claiming him to be one of the most productive artists in the program and commenting on the large numbers of requests for his watercolor paintings. In addition to producing the watercolors, Zornes also designed and painted two murals for projects funded through the W.P.A. art project. One mural, produced for the Treasury Relief Art Project adorns the walls of the United States Post Office in Claremont, California and depicts scenes of the Pomona Valley. The other depicts Texas landscape subjects and was mounted in the post office at El Campo, Texas. Both of these murals were painted with oils on canvas and are still on display at the post office locations.

The 1930s closed with several major projects. For almost six months Zornes worked assisting Millard Sheets on a monumental mural project for the Golden Gate International Exposition in San Francisco. Together they painted six detailed panels twenty-five feet high and twenty feet wide. These murals hung on the walls of the ''Court of the Flowers'' display during the 1939 to 1940 Worlds Fair on Treasure Island. In addition, Zornes produced several easel paintings that were also exhibited at the World's Fair and painted a series of watercolors for one-man shows which were scheduled to take place in 1940.

In 1941 Zornes became president of the California Water Color Society. His primary job was to arrange the annual exhibition of watercolors by

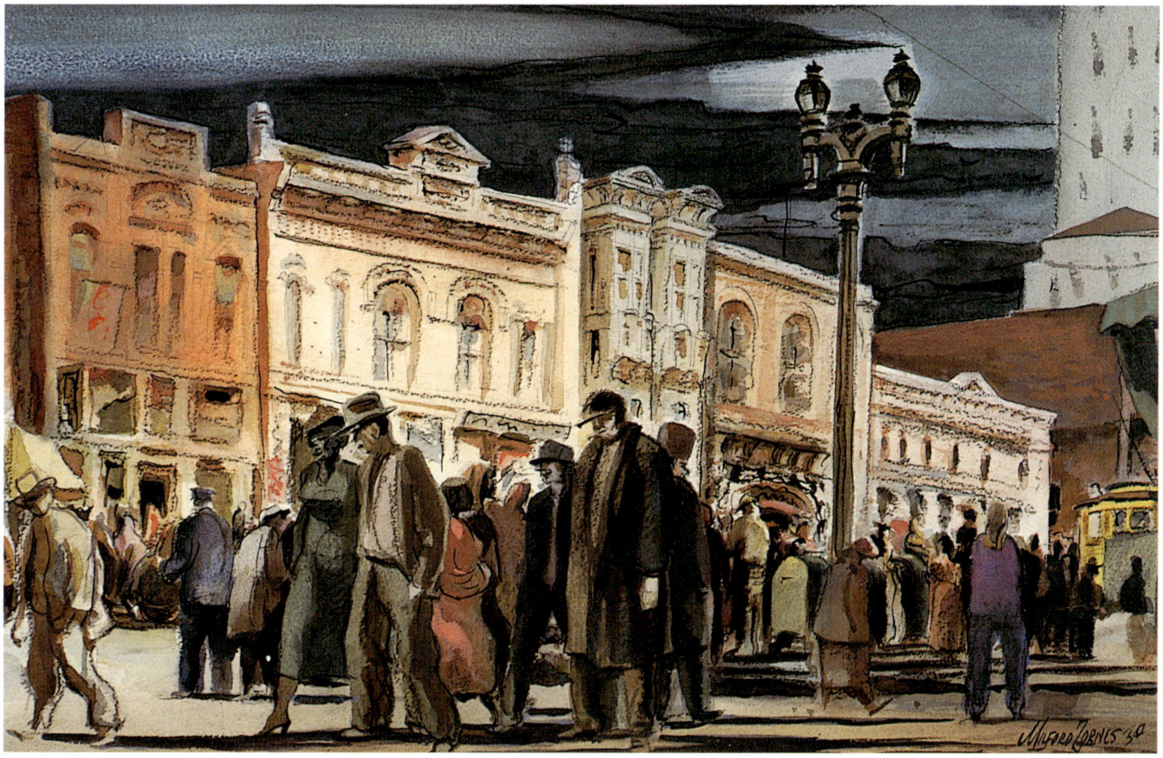

Downtown L.A.. 1939 Watercolor 15 x 22 in.

Society members and see to the promotional publicity. All the previous annual exhibitions had opened in Los Angeles, so Zornes decided to make a change. He arranged for the twenty-first annual exhibition to premier in the San Francisco Museum of Art, then travel south to the Los Angeles County Museum and then go north again to the Santa Barbara Museum of Art. In addition to works by the regular members, the Society was also presenting watercolors by specially invited guest artists during this era. Yasuo Kuniyoshi, Paul Cadmus, Clarence Carter, and William Gropper exhibited in this particular traveling show. After viewing the paintings, Los Angeles *Times* art critic Arthur Millier declared: "For the best watercolor show ever offered here, make the trip to the museum."

When America entered World War II and went on a war time economy, the California Style watercolor movement came to an abrupt stop. Many of the members became soldiers and art exhibitions were often canceled. The public had survival on their minds, and art was not a high priority. While this had a stifling affect on Zornes art career he had much to be grateful for. In ten short years he went from being a student artist to a nationally recognized watercolorist, muralist and teacher, with works in many notable museums and private collections throughout the country. In many ways this had been a Golden Era for Zornes and many of the other California watercolor artists.

2

1942–1950

"The truth is, I sketch incessantly as a way of observation, but for me, on site painting, as much as possible, is a continuing necessity. I need the impact of subject matter while I am in the act of painting. The immediate association of the things and places that I depict through technique of design, makes the adventure of seeing and artistic discovery a kind of whole experience."

— M.Z.

With the new decade Zornes' life changed. While teaching at the Otis Art Institute he met Pat Palmer and in November of 1942 they were married. At that time she was working for Warner Brothers painting cels for animated films and cartoons and Zornes was working on an animated film titled "Victory Through Air Power" at the Walt Disney Studios. Just as the newlyweds settled into a home in Los Angeles, Zornes was drafted into the U.S. Army.

Zornes was first stationed at March Field in Riverside, California where he completed engineers training. After reviewing a list of his qualifications the Army selected Zornes to be an official war artist and assigned him to duty in India, Burma and China. In 1944 he wrote the following account of this experience.

"Having worked as a professional artist for many years before my induction into the Army, I was, upon the completion of my basic training, selected by a committee acting for the War Department and given an assignment to come overseas in the capacity of Artist painter to do a series of painting and drawings for the War Department record.

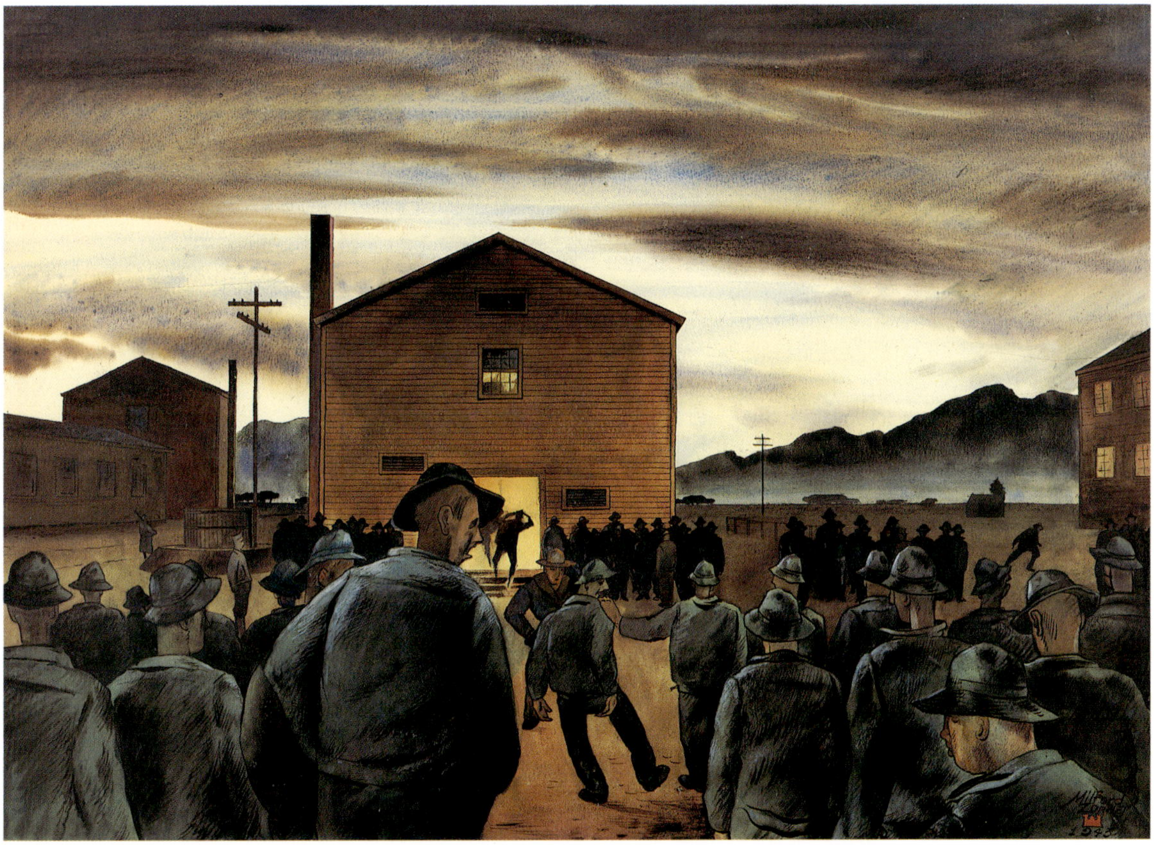

Revelie. 1943 Watercolor 22 x 30 in. Mike and Susan Verbal Collection.

For this work, I was equipped by the Army Engineers acting on orders from the Adjutant General's Office, War Department, Washington, D.C. I was issued a camera and allowed to purchase, by vouchers through procurement offices in San Francisco, painting materials to the value of three hundred dollars.

On 23 July 1945, I sailed from Wilmington, California on a Liberty ship. Sixty two days later I arrived in India. While at sea, in accordance with my instructions, I painted pictures: scenes aboard ship, sketches of gunners and seamen at work, Army cargo.

Upon reaching New Dehli, I learned that original War Department orders had been rescinded and that I was to be re-assigned according to my abilities. I was re-assigned to Theater Special Services Section. A general order issued 22 November 1945 by the Theater Special Service Office reads as follows:

1. This directs you to utilize your exceptional abilities as an artist and photographer to portray pictorially the activities of Special Service and Red Cross work in the China Burma India Theater.

2. Under this assignment you will, of your own initiative, as well as under command of the Theater Special Service Officer, prepare a graphic series of pictures in pencil, crayon, water colors and/or oils depicting Special Service as it pertains to the enlisted man.

a. In this connection you are granted latitude to develop such background material on life, customs and architecture in the theater as you deem necessary to accomplish your mission.

3. All such materials developed will be turned over to the Army through the Theater Special Service Officer for disposition and use.

Under this order, I have traveled and done work as detailed below:In the vicinity of New Delhi—paintings, sketches and photographs of native life and village life of Indian people; sketches of Indian people of this area; the life of American soldiers in the Indian setting; the building of barracks by Indian Labor; Indian customs, shops, homes, etc.

During February, March and the early part of April of this year I was in Assam, on Ledo Road and in Burma. There I made pictures of men, barracks, machinery at work, jungle landscapes activities on the Burma front. I lived with Troop carriers, Engineers, Special Service Units, anti-aircraft units, always sketching and becoming acquainted with the activities of these units.

On the 5th of April I returned to New Delhi from Assam. I then prepared work for exhibition in an Allied Art and Photographic Exhibition held at the Imperial Hotel in New Delhi April 15th to April 17th, 1944. Proceeds from the sale of catalogues for this exhibition were given to the Viceroys War Purposes fund. I submitted 18 paintings for this exhibition and received praise personally from the Viceroy and Lady Wavell who attended the exhibition.

On April 23rd, I took paintings to Bombay where I submitted them for exhibition in The All India United Nations Services Art Exhibition organized by the Bombay Art Society. Prizes were offered for this Exhibition and I was the winner of the Presidents Prize for the best work in this Show on my watercolor painting *The Jungle*, painted on the Ledo Road.

Subsequent activities have been the submitting of sketches for publication in the C.B.I. Roundup. A page of my drawings done on Ledo Road were printed in that newspaper in the issue for 1 June 1944.

On a trip to the American Army rest camp at Khanspur, I painted a series of water colors that depict, in landscape subjects, that part of India, and I did many drawings of the people who live there in the Frontier Provinces.

I am making studies for a decoration to be painted in the Heaquarters Company Day Room. These studies constitute a part of my series of paintings and the decoration will be executed under my direction with the help of other men of the Headquarters Company.

At the present date, I am completing pictures in preparation for an exhibition in the Red Cross Show in Calcutta where I will go the latter part of this month.

It is my purpose to continue my travel and study of this Theater. It is my aim to complete as many paintings as I possibly can. It is my desire that my paintings be used exclusively for exhibition in Service Clubs and such places where enlisted men can see them and derive a maximum of such benefit as they may have to give. It is my hope that I may report to the War Department with a comprehensive and worthwhile Artist story

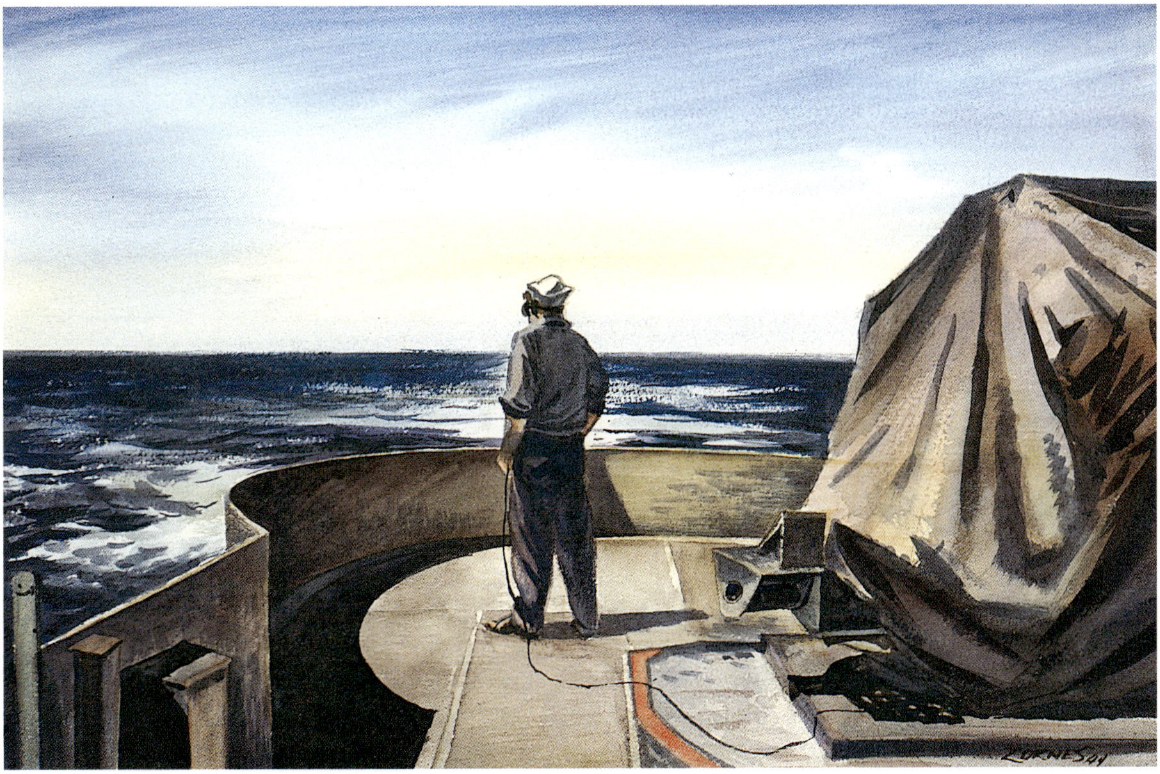

Gunner on Watch. 1944 Watercolor 15 x 22 in.

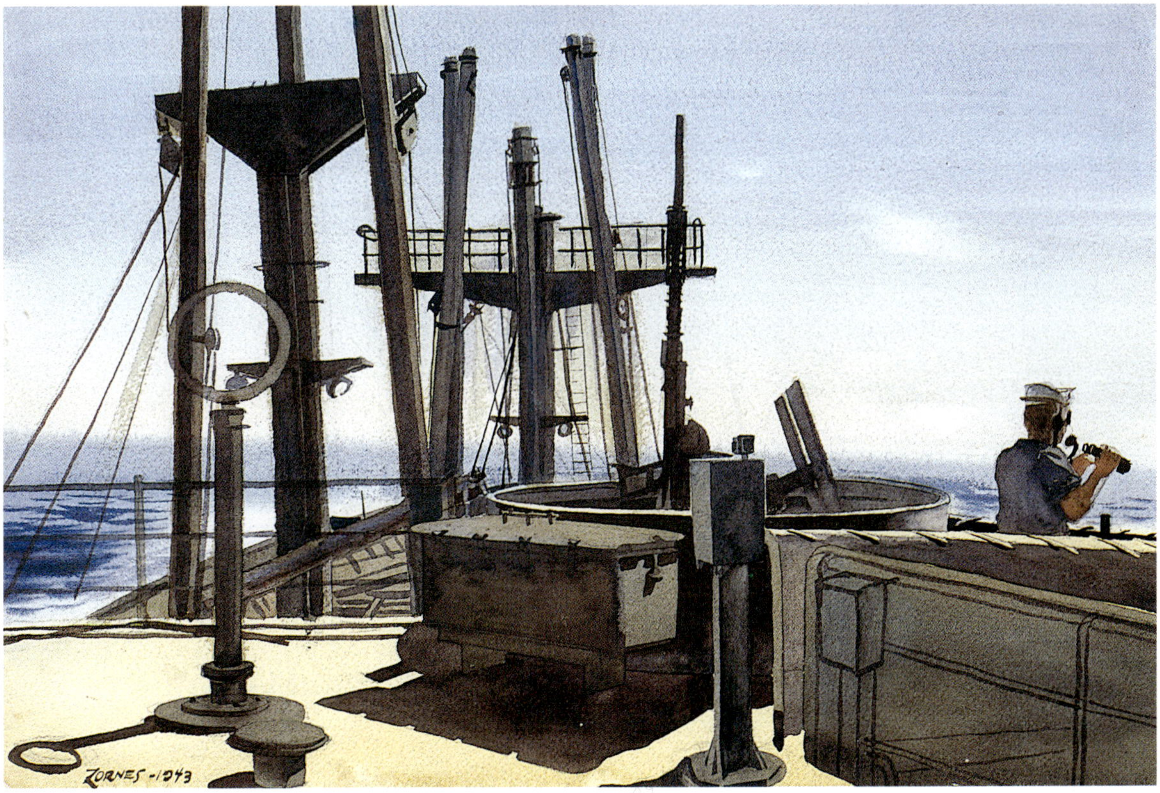

Liberty Ship. 1943 Watercolor 15 x 22 in.

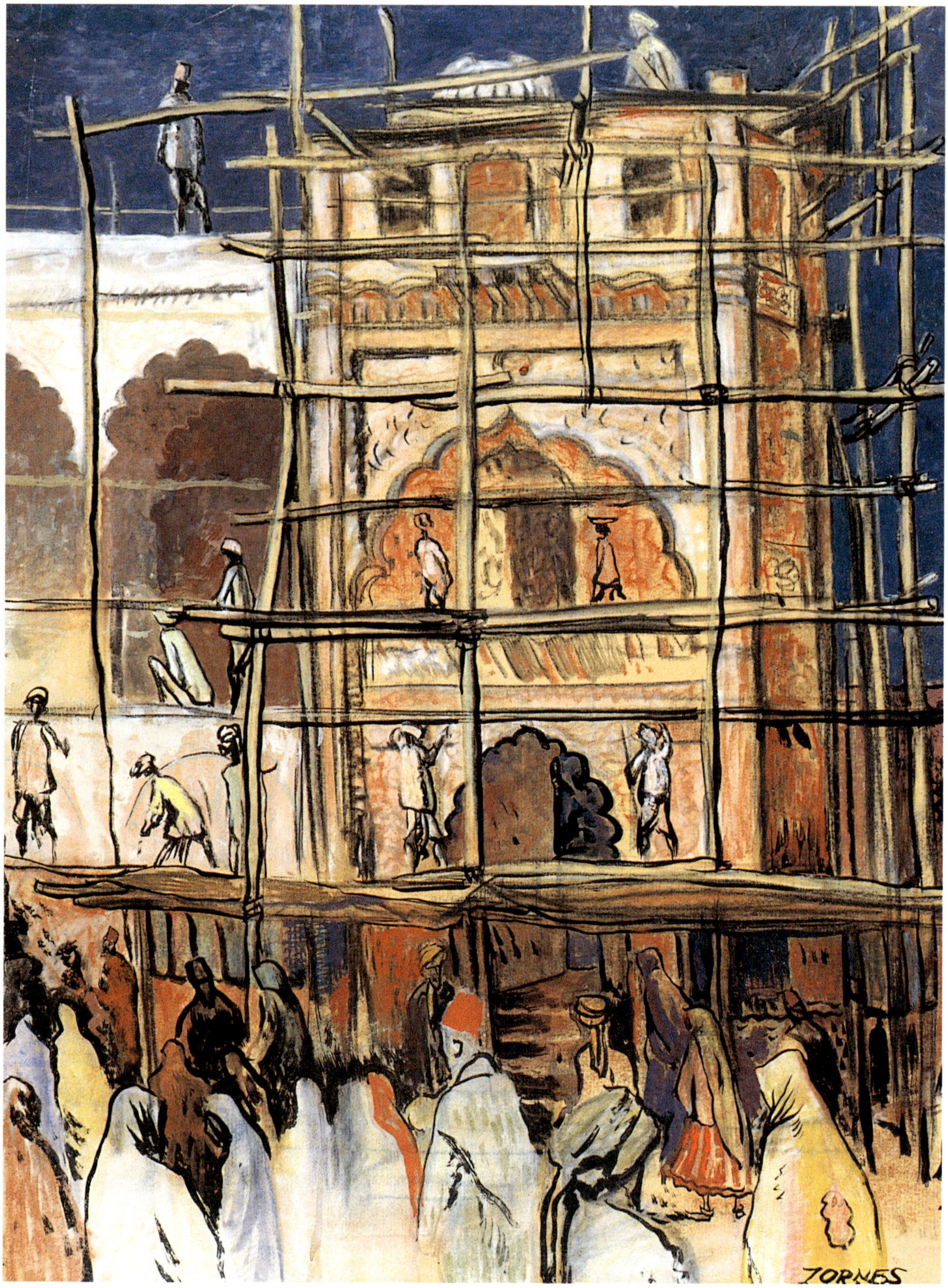

India. 1943 Watercolor 22 x 15 in. Salley Curtis Collection.

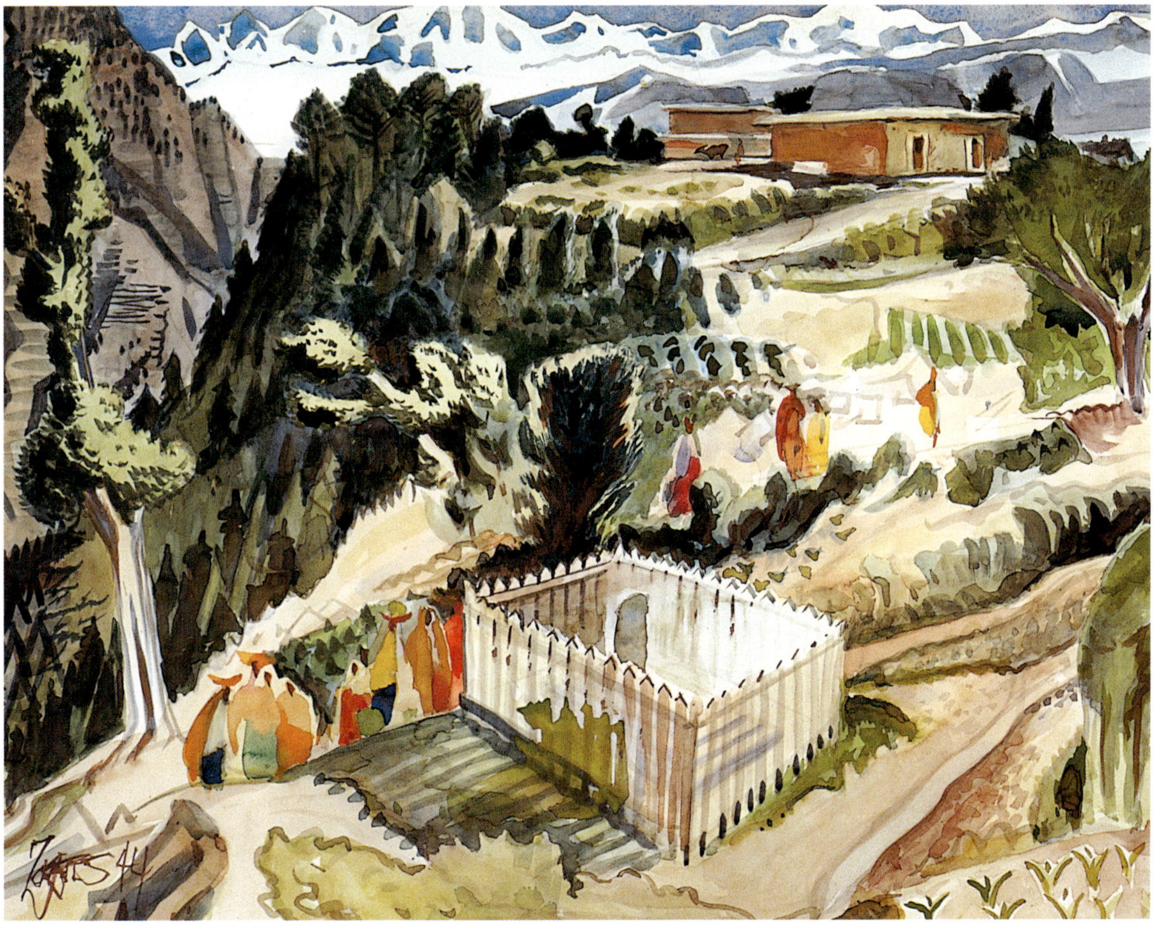

The Grave of Mir Hosui Khow. 1944 Watercolor 22 x 30 in.

of the C.B.I. Theater. As an artist who has concerned himself with the meaning of pictures as well as with the techniques, then I may, with skill and understanding paint and write about India, China, and Burma. If properly presented in exhibitions and publications these efforts should have worthwhile significance in furthering knowledge and interest in these countries.

I want my pictures to be the public property of the men of the Army and eventually of American civilians as well. I believe literally in the old adage that a picture is worth a thousand words, and as a painter I firmly believe that painting and drawing are mediums that have greater possibilities than photography. With this in mind, I make pictures all the time wherever I go that tell about the things I see. To whom it may concern, I respectfully present this report together with the following detailed list of completed works and an outline of future travel that will help accomplish my assignment and purpose.''

Shortly after this was written World War II ended. Zornes finished up his drawings and paintings and turned them over to the United States

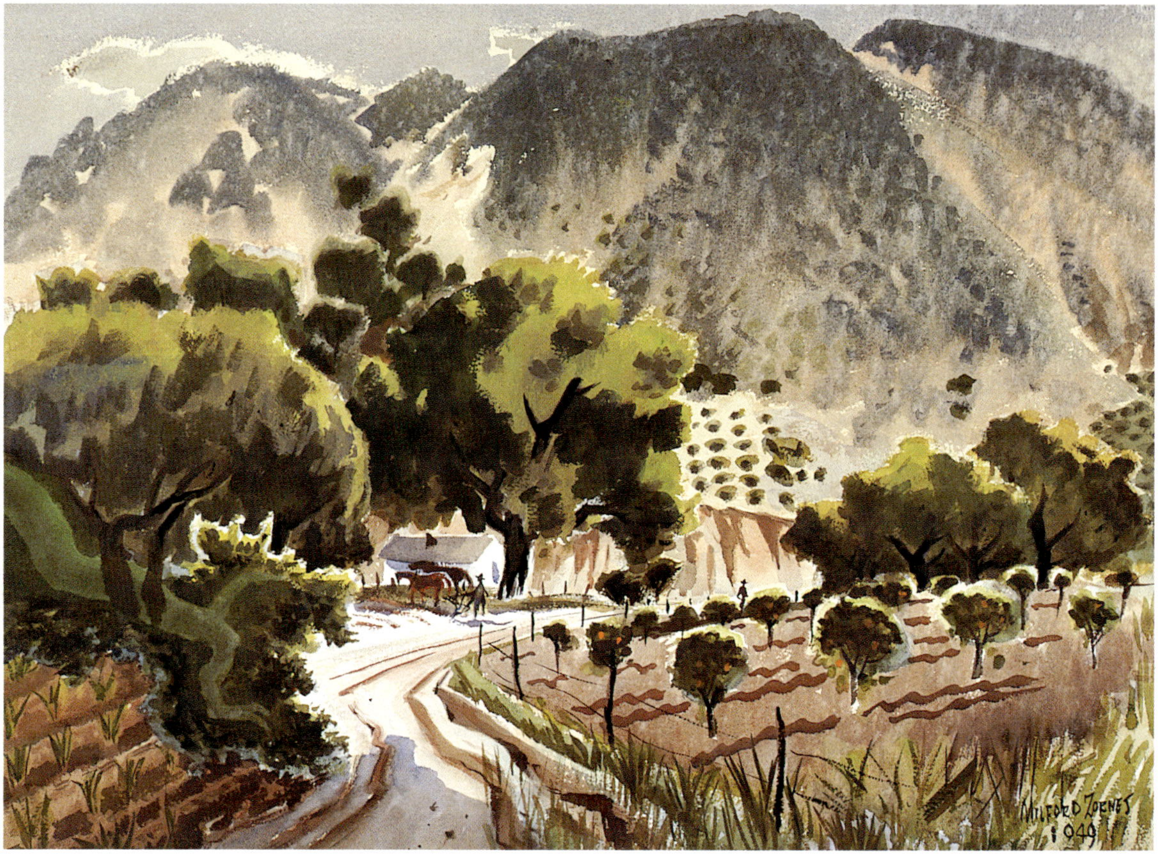

Canyon Farm. 1949 Watercolor 22 x 30 in.

Government Historical Properties section. He was flown back to America and released from duty in the service.

When Zornes returned to Los Angeles he was greeted by his wife Pat and their daughter Maria Patricia, born while he was overseas. A teaching job at the Otis Art Institute was also awaiting him. Vast numbers of soldiers were returning home and many were enrolling in art school on the G.I. Bill. Art classes at every school were filled, so experienced art teachers were in great demand. This job required Zornes to spend two days each week teaching painting classes. The rest of his time was spent painting on location and exhibiting his art.

For several months the Zornes family continued to live in Los Angeles but in November they moved to Nipomo, California. This scenic farm community is located on the coast near the central California city of Santa Maria. The surrounding countryside and beaches provided Zornes with a wealth of inspiring subjects to paint. He worked with both oils and watercolors during this era and chose to depict regional scenes similar to those produced in the 1930s.

Also during this period Zornes traveled to Tuscon, Arizona where Maynard Dixon was producing two murals for the Santa Fe ticket office in Chicago. As it turned out Dixon died before completing this project, so at the request of his widow, Edith Hamlin Dixon, Zornes and Buck

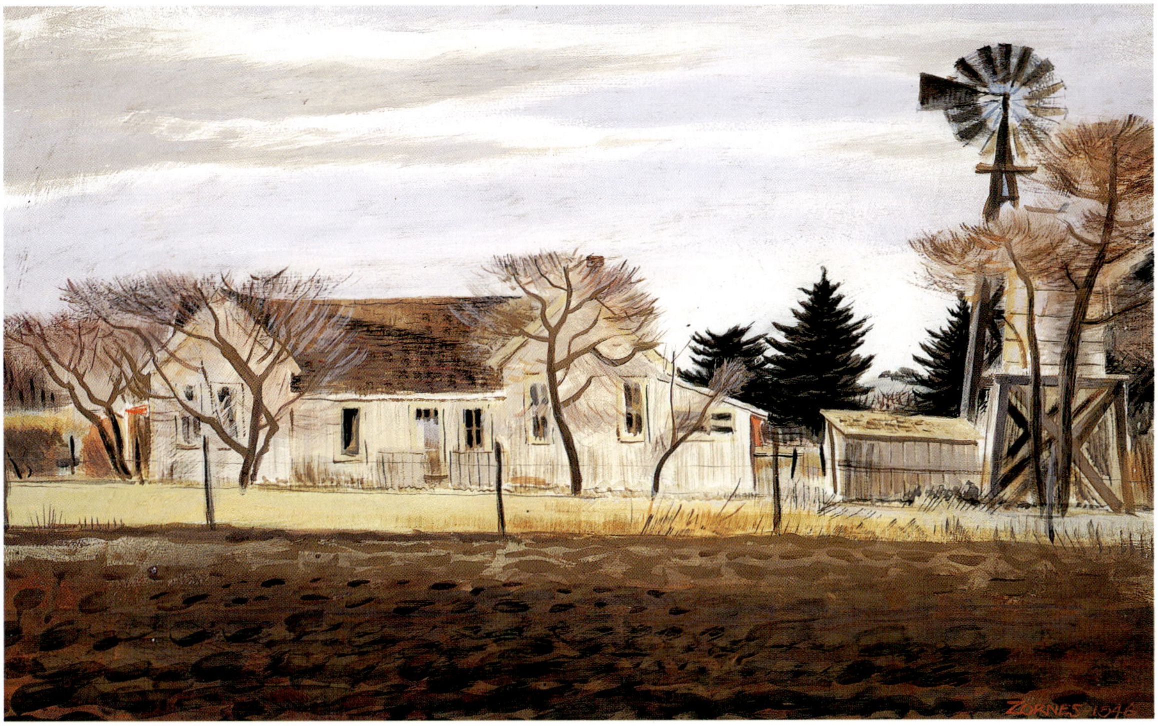

Farm at Nipomo. 1946 Casein 22 x 30 in. Courtesy Gary Breitweiser.

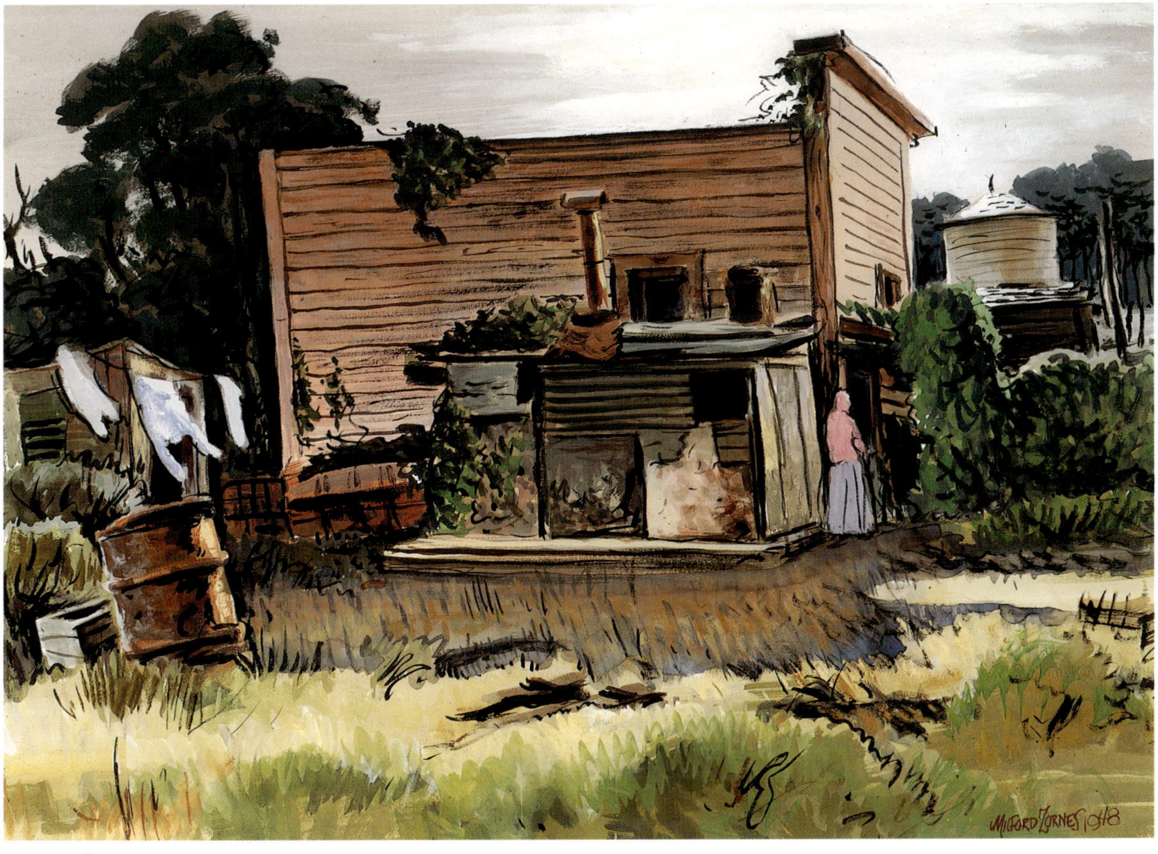

Afternoon in Summerland. 1948 Watercolor 21 x 27½ in.
John and Nancy Weare Collection.

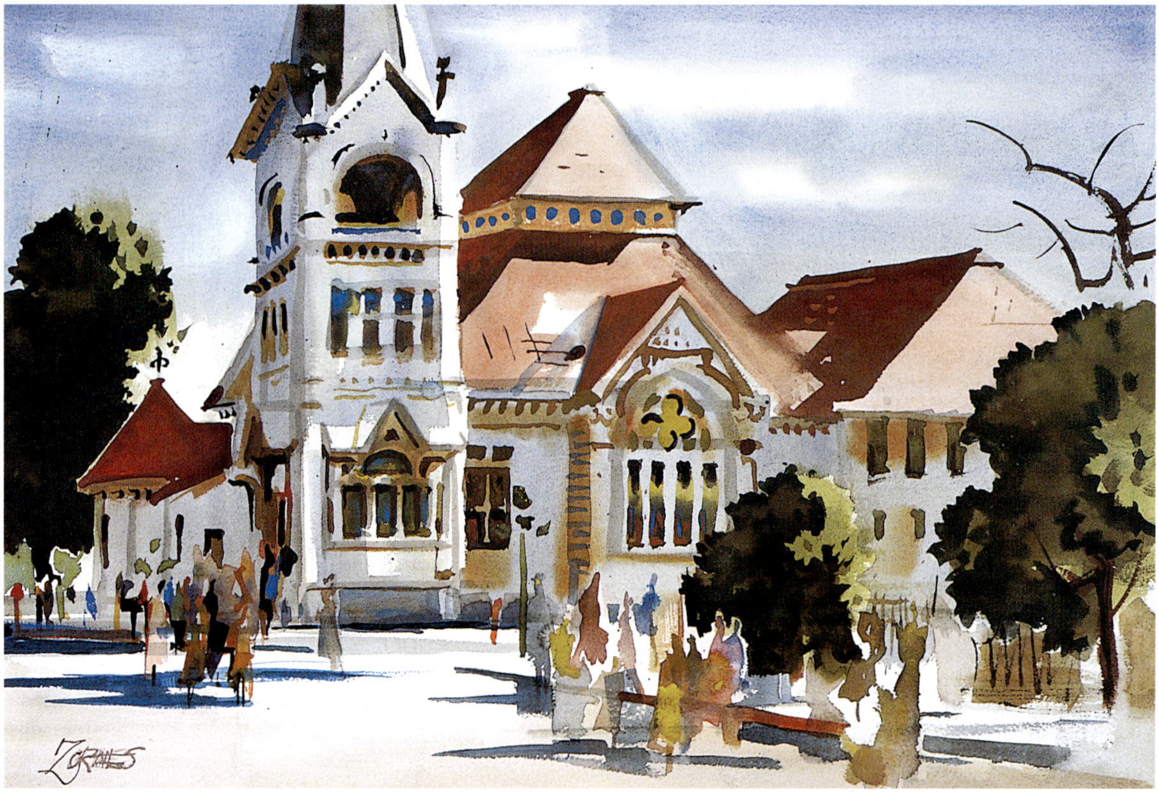

Pomona Sunday. 1949 Watercolor 22 x 30 in. Glen and Pam Knowles Collection.

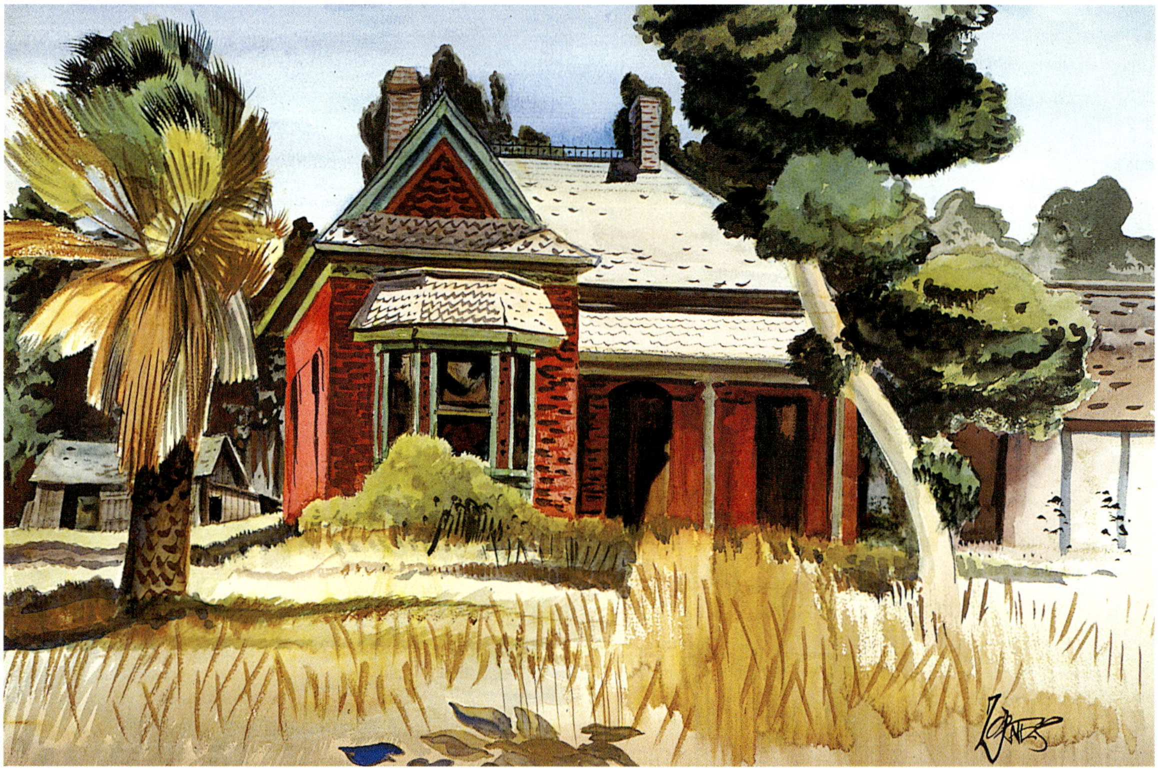

The Old House. 1949 Watercolor 22 x 30 in. Courtesy David Howard Fine Arts.

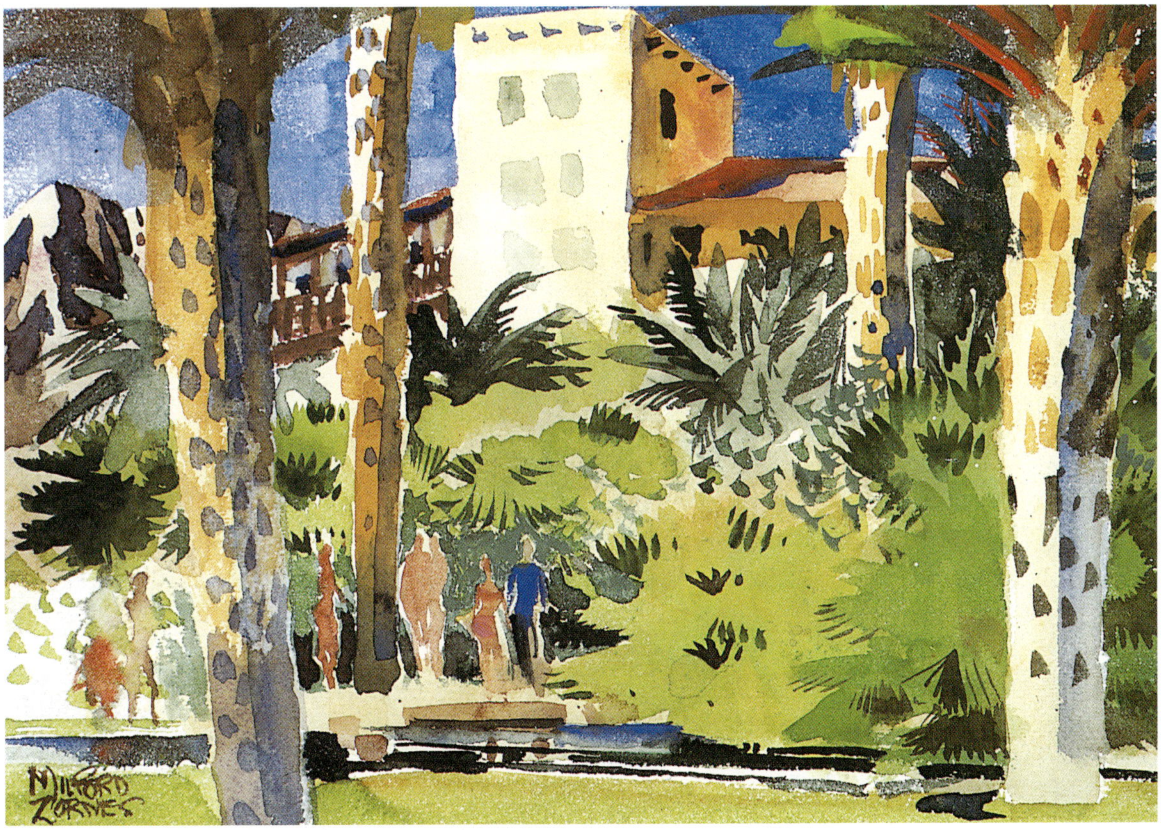

Grand Ave. L.A. 1949 Watercolor 11 x 15 in.

Weaver helped her finish the murals. Both murals, painted with oils on canvas, depict classic southwestern scenes. One is ten feet high by thirty five feet long and depicts a section of the Grand Canyon. The other, ten feet high by fifteen feet long, features a Taos Pueblo scene with Indians in their native habitat.

In 1946 Zornes was offered a teaching position at his alma mater, Pomona College which he accepted. He sold his farm in Nipomo and moved his family to Claremont. At this time Scripps College, located next to Pomona College, had a unique art program developed by Millard Sheets. Several prominent artist/teachers, including Henry Lee McFee, Albert Stewart, Richard Petterson, Sueo Serisawa, Rex Brandt and Phil Paradise, taught classes there. This same year Alfredo Ramos Martinez, an outstanding Mexican artist also came to Claremont to paint a mural. It was an exciting era as this small city established itself as a West Coast center for the arts.

The prospect of sharing a key role in the development of this project excited Zornes and inspired him to set up an outstanding art program for Pomona College. His classes were primarily painting instruction. Students divided their time between studying academics in the classroom and painting landscape scenes outdoors on location. While Zornes personally specialized in painting relatively conservative works using transparent

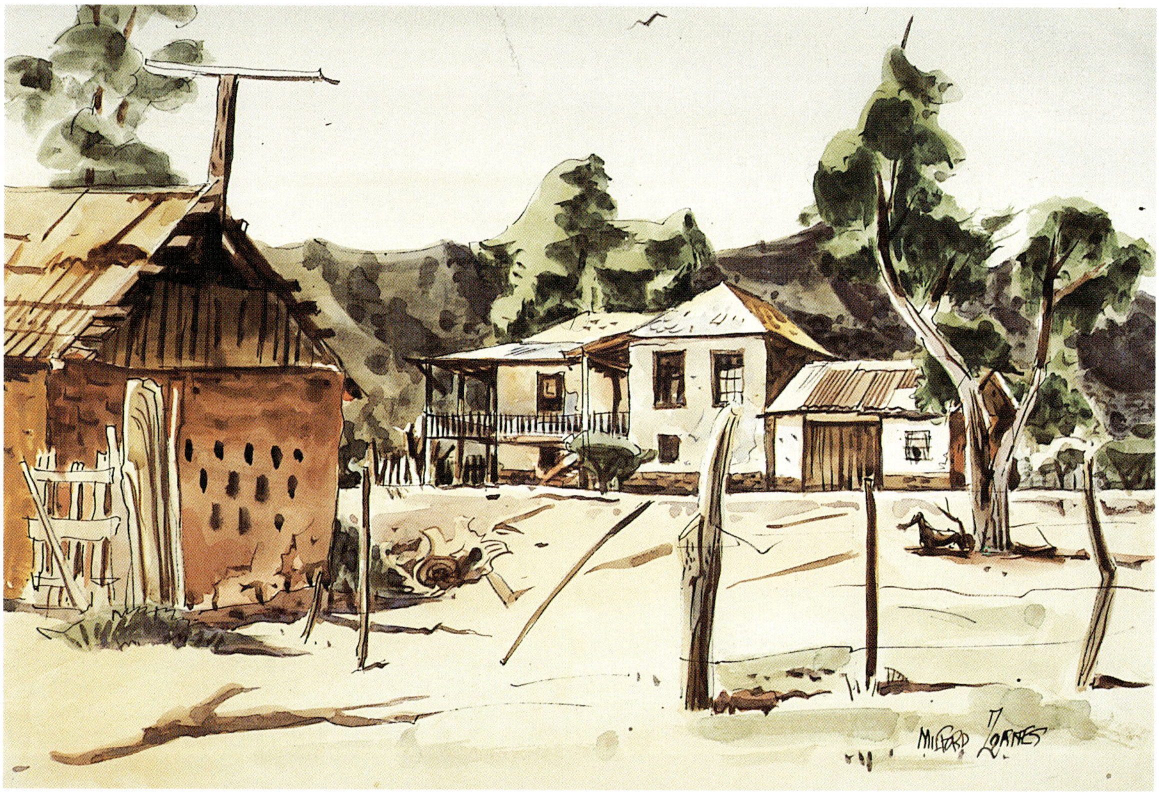

Guadalupe. 1949 Watercolor 18 x 28 in. Courtesy Barbara Beretich.

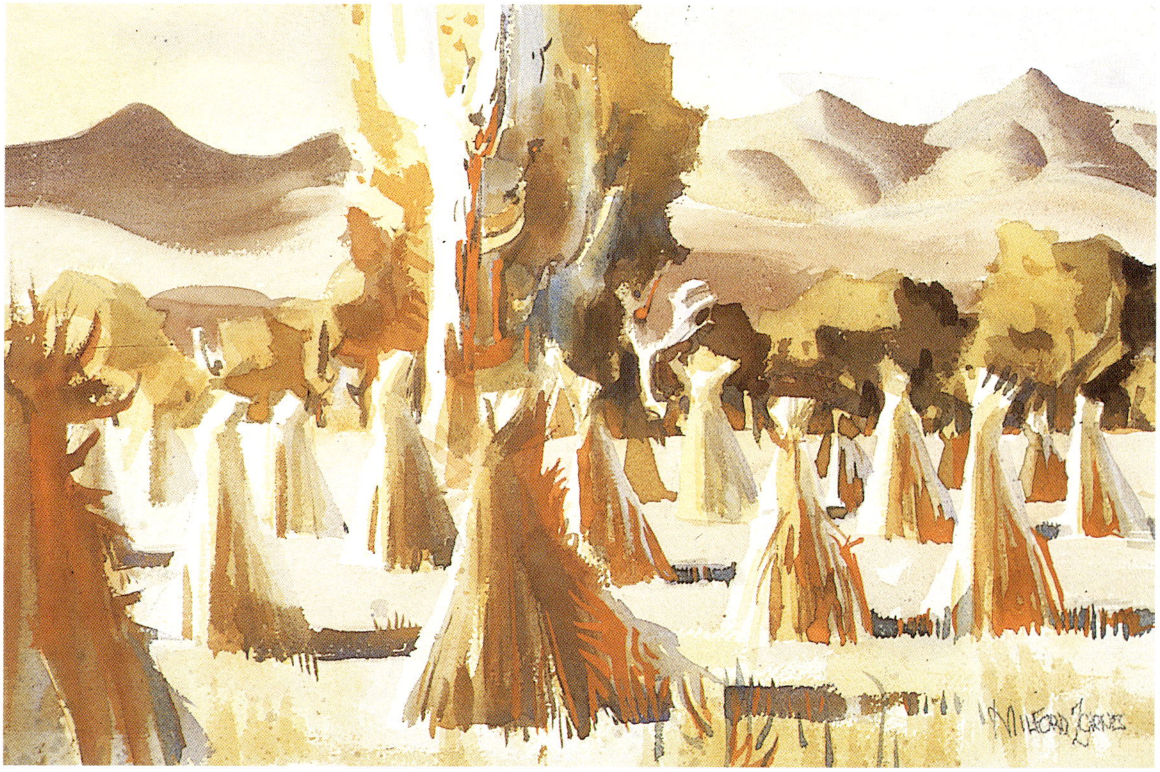

Autumn. 1948 Watercolor 15 x 22 in.

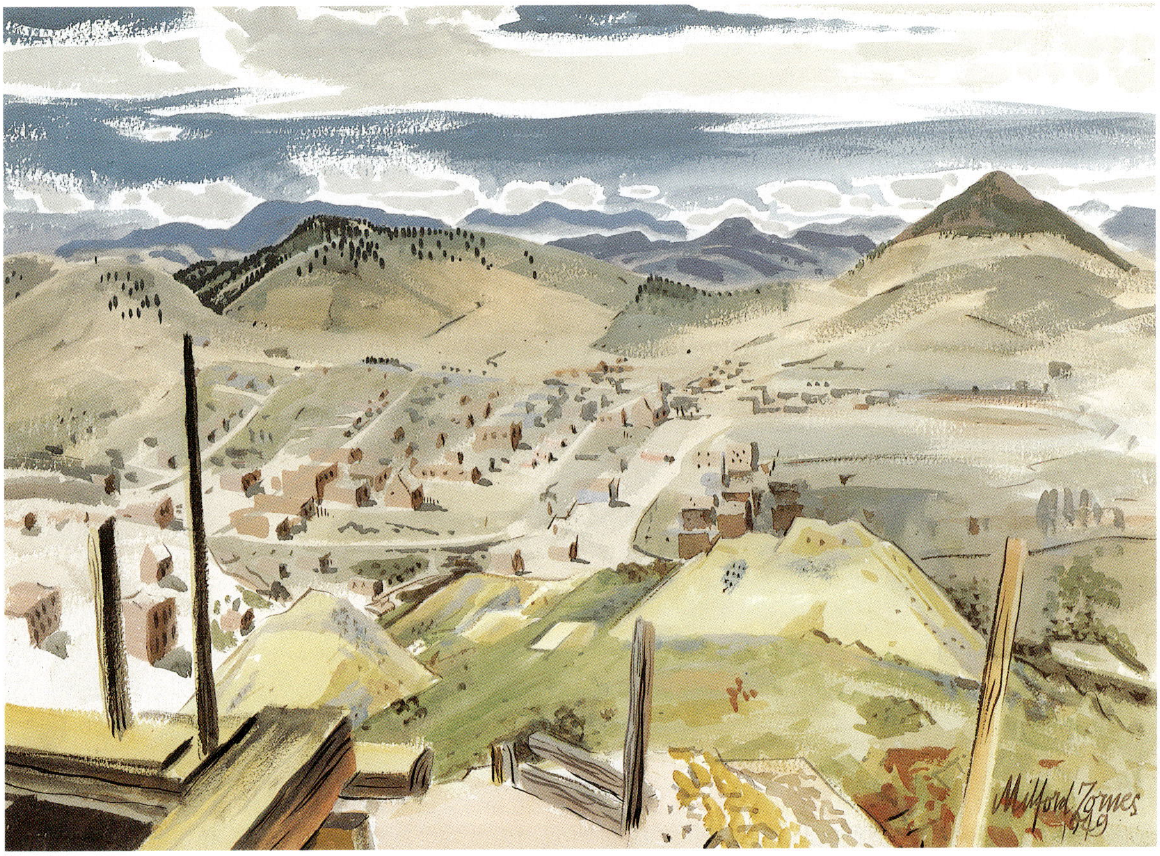

Cripple Creek. 1949 Watercolor 22 x 30 in. Mike and Susan Verbal Collection.

watercolors, his students were encouraged to experiment with varied painting mediums and with abstract or non-objective styles. Out of these classes emerged several well known artists including Roger Kuntz and Robert E. Wood.

Each summer and on extended school breaks, Zornes would travel to a chosen location and spent several weeks to a month painting a series of related works for one-man exhibitions. Two well known shows from this period include works painted on location in Alaska (1948) and Cripple Creek, Colorado (1949). Both of these shows traveled to various museums and galleries in California. When the Alaskan series opened at the Rotunda Gallery in downtown San Francisco, the following review was printed in a local newspaper. "Crags, glaciers, waterways and towns of Alaska are Zornes principal theme. They provide a grand and interesting subject. Zornes builds them on a proper scale, keeping their natural appearance, but working them out in a fine, sweeping and imaginative spirit that is clearly his own."

This is typical of the many reviews that Zornes' exhibitions received. While opinions often varied between critics regarding the subjects Zornes chose to depict, they consistantly agreed and approved of, his creative approaches to handling the watercolor medium.

3

1950–1963

"Having long since made the not so startling discovery that art is not the best choice of professions by which to get rich, my belief is that one becomes an artist because of a certain independence of spirit and to give up that independence is to give up the real reward of being an artist."

—M.Z.

Although most of Zornes' paintings from the 1930s and 1940s were watercolors depicting landscapes and cityscapes, on occasion he also received commissions to paint portraits. It was while completing a portrait of Lou Anne Paul, one of his former students, that he became acquainted with her father's position as vice president of a large construction firm. After talking in depth with Mr. Paul about his business Zornes found that the company was involved with the construction of an Air Force Base in a remote Arctic region near Thule, Greenland. Since childhood Zornes had desired to visit the Arctic and while this visit was not to be in the capacity of an explorer as he had dreamed, he resigned from his teaching position at Pomona College and became an employee of the North Atlantic Constructors.

Between 1950 and 1955 Zornes spent six to eight months of each year living, working and painting in Thule, Greenland. He stated: "When the crew of 6,000 men moved into Greenland, we instantly created the most populated single city in the whole Arctic region. I worked with the surveyors on laying out the base. Since it was light 24 hours a day I found time to paint and sketch pictures of the surrounding landscape. I brought

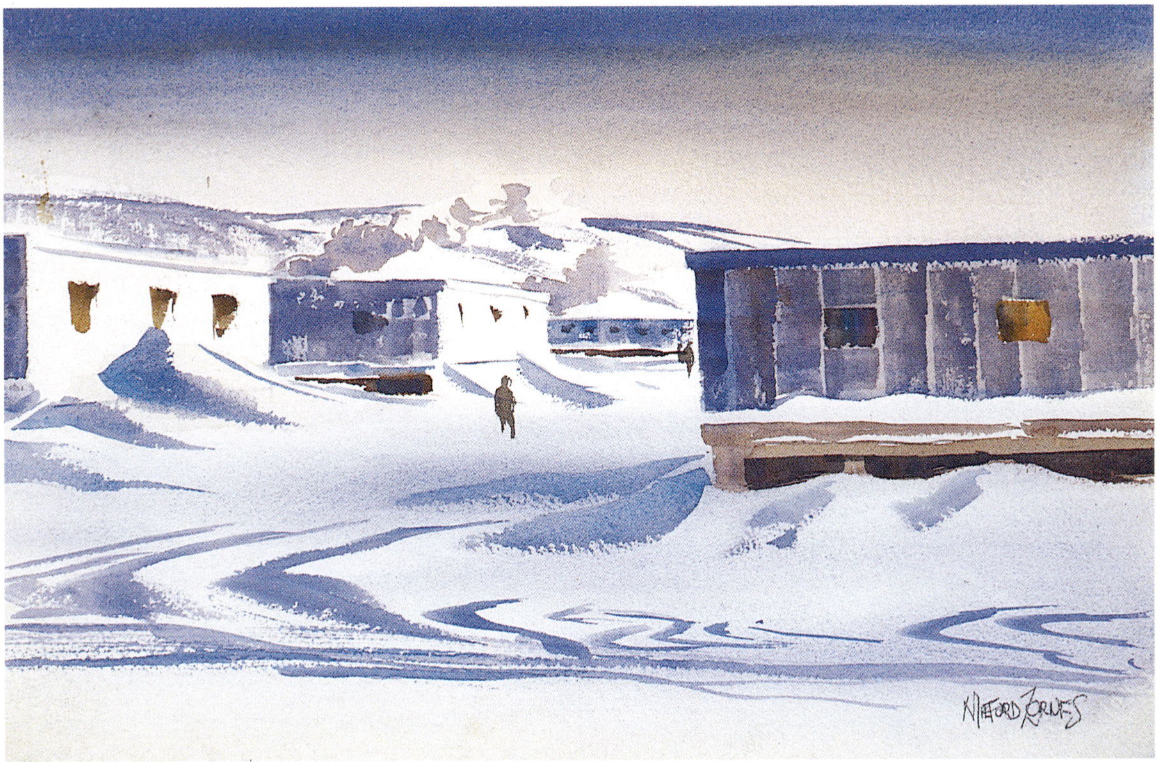

Spring at Thule. 1953 Watercolor 15 x 22 in.

watercolors with me but in some periods encountered an unusual problem; the watercolors and brush would immediately freeze making it impossible to paint. I knew if alcohol was added to the water this would help, but due to company restrictions on liquor, alcohol was hard to find. I soon discovered hair tonic contained alcohol, so I added it to my painting water and resolved the problem. It was an exciting place to work and paint. The landscape was so very sparse and the unusual lines and patterns formed by the wind blowing over the snow and ice made unique subjects for my paintings. I'd go back there in a second if the opportunity arose."

While Zornes enjoyed this job and welcomed the change, it was only possible to live in this type of isolation and cold weather for up to eight months a year. The remaining time was spent with his wife and daughter or traveling throughout the southwest and into Mexico. The bulk of Zornes' watercolor paintings from this era depict scenes from these regions and many, particularly those done in Greenland, brought much attention when they went on exhibition.

Having completed his assignment in Greenland, Zornes returned to Claremont in 1955 and began seeking part time employment to support his family. The paintings he produced brought in some income but since he could not find a gallery that he could work with, it was not enough. Zornes recalled: "In those days many of the gallery owners wanted to control what I painted. They would demand pictures of certain subjects,

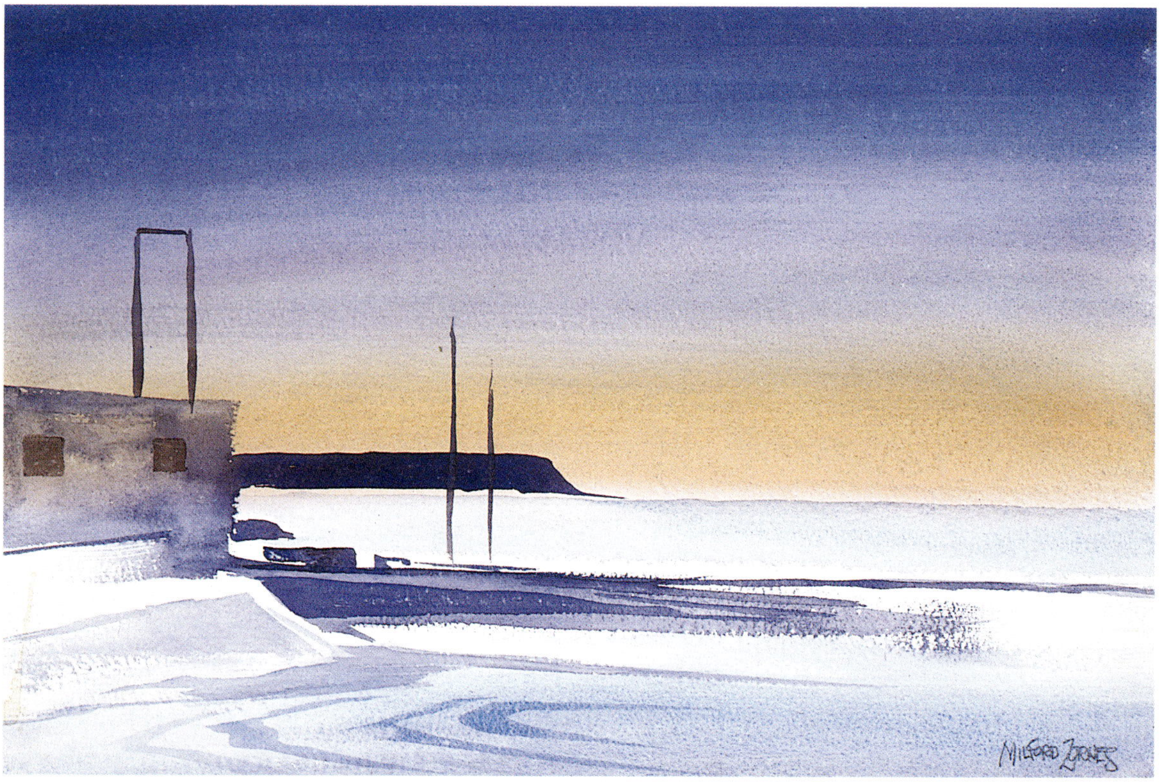

Greenland Dawn. 1953 Watercolor 15 x 22 in.

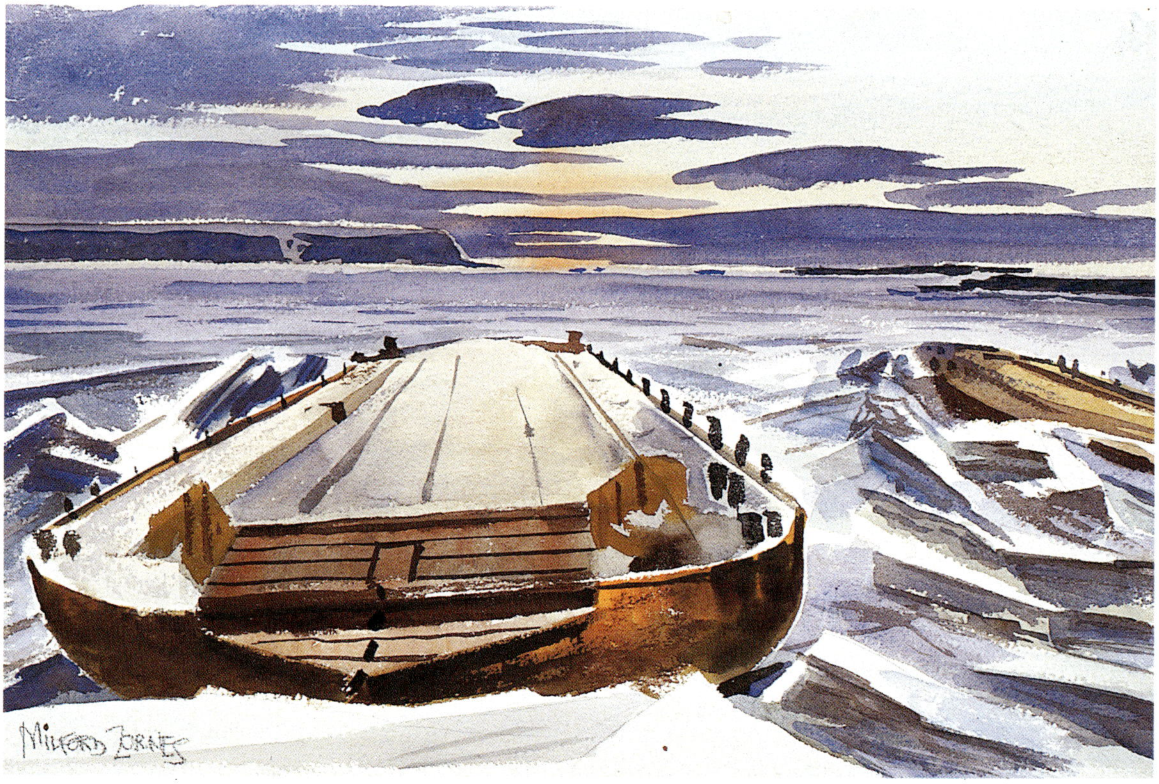

Landing Barge at Thule. 1953 Watercolor 15 x 22 in.

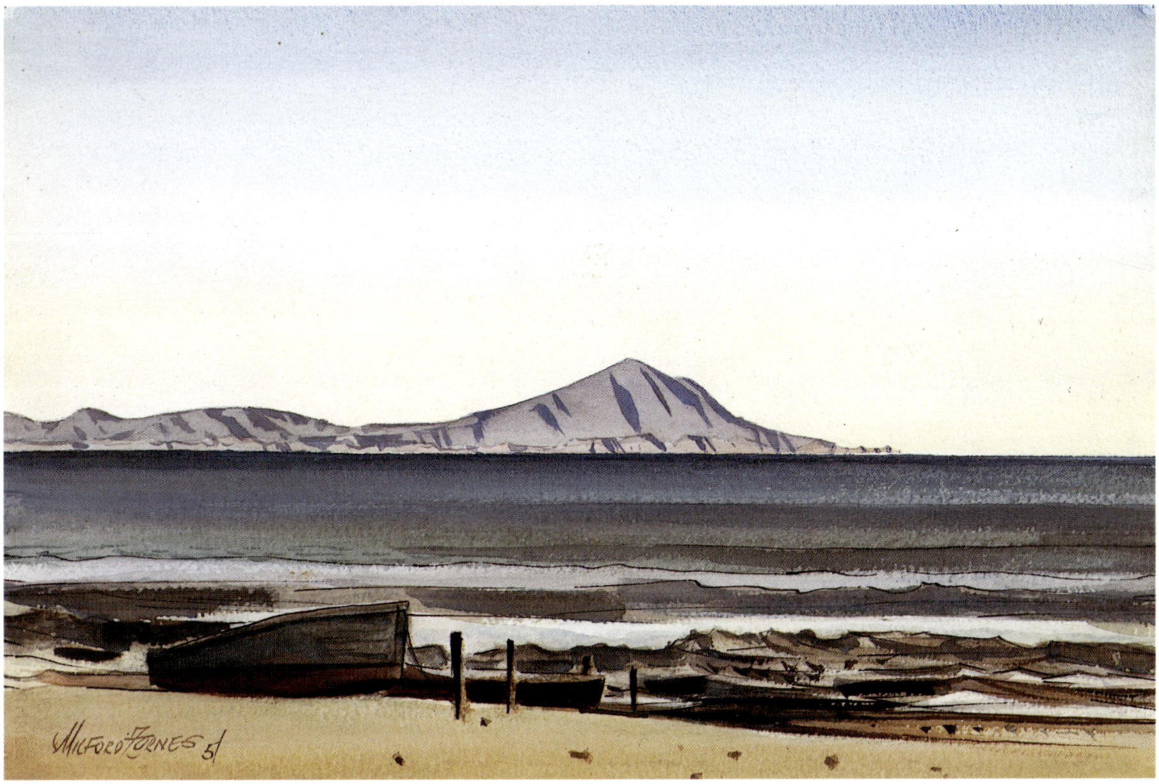

Ensenada. 1951 Watercolor 15 x 22 in. Courtesy David Howard Fine Arts.

painted a certain way and this was unacceptable to me. So, I simply refused to deal with them. Instead I chose to teach or work part time to support my wife and daughter. This allowed me to paint whatever I wanted and continually explore and experiment, with no concern whatsoever about whether the art would sell or not."

Zornes found part time employment as art director for the Padua Hills Theater in Claremont. This theater was well known during this period for its productions by the Mexican Players. It was built in the hills above the city and was designed in a classic Mexican/Spanish type of architecture. The performances introduced Southern California audiences to authentic Mexcian folk theater productions and musical performances.

Zornes took on the job of designing posters, programs and promotional materials for these shows. In addition, he directed the presentation of art exhibitions inside the theater and an art festival on the grounds. Each year he would present an exhibition of his most recent works and schedule one-man exhibits by other prominent artists including Phil Dike, Millard Sheets, Rex Brandt, and Phil Paradise. The art festivals featured painters, sculptors, potters and craftsman from the Claremont area and drew crowds of interested residents from the Los Angeles region.

Working for the theater and teaching an art class in Pasadena left Zornes with at least half of each week to pursue his location painting. He fre-

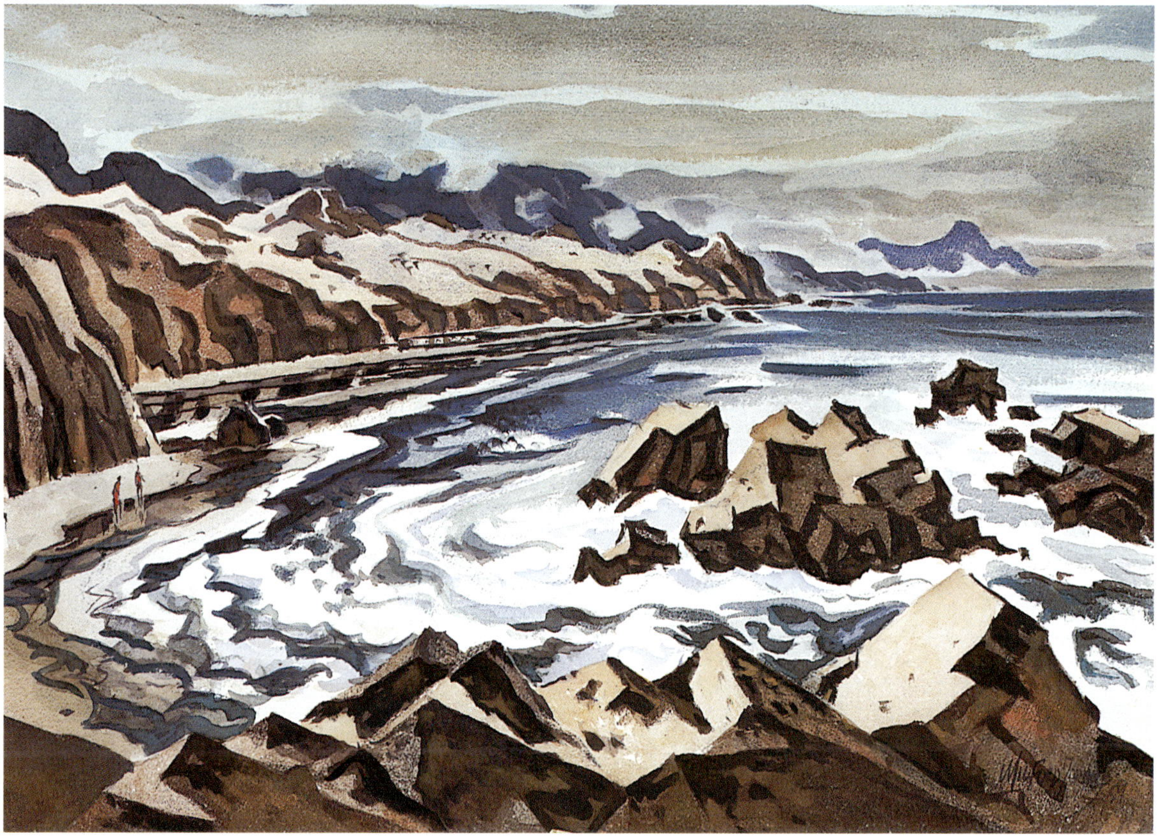

At Point Sol. 1959 Watercolor 22 x 30 in.

quently got in his car with plenty of art supplies and headed out to explore interesting new areas with challenging subjects. With the new freeway systems being installed in California throughout the late 1950s, his one-day painting excursions had many possibilities. From his home in Claremont he could travel to Mexico in less than three hours. The beach at Laguna took just a little more than one hour and the remote desert region beyond Palm Springs about two hours. These and other similar regions became favored places for Zornes to set up and paint.

Zornes was working to reaffirm his position as a vital part of the West Coast art community. While he was away in Greenland and traveling during the first half of the 1950s, the California art scene had gone through drastic changes. Most of the 1930s and 1940s era watercolor artists from the original group had gone their separate ways. Paul Sample, Barse Miller, Lee Blair, Hardie Gramatky and Dong Kingman all moved to the eastern United States. Tom Craig stopped painting and set up a hybrid flower business and many of the artists that did stay in California were busy pursuing careers and raising families. While most of these artists continued to submit paintings to the annual watercolor exhibitions throughout America, the comradery and sharing of ideas while painting together had vanished.

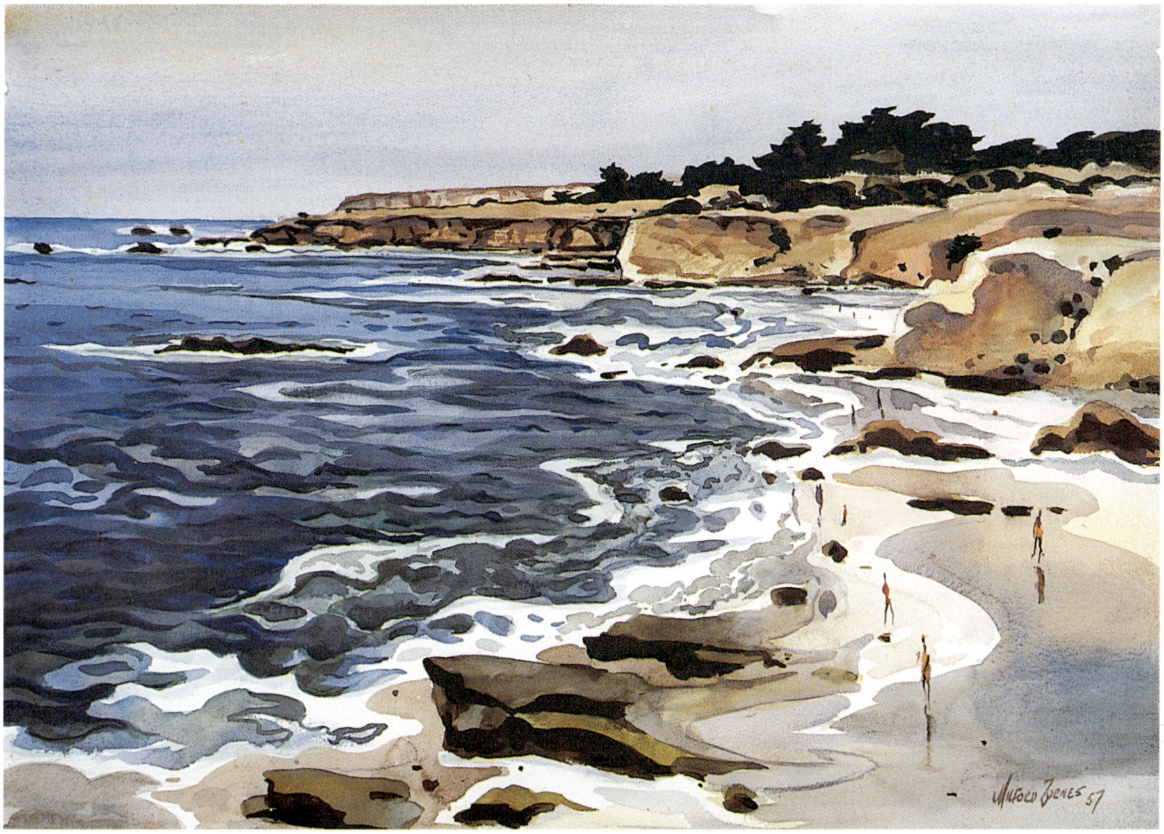

Laguna Shoreline. Watercolor 22 x 30 in. Greg Young Collection.

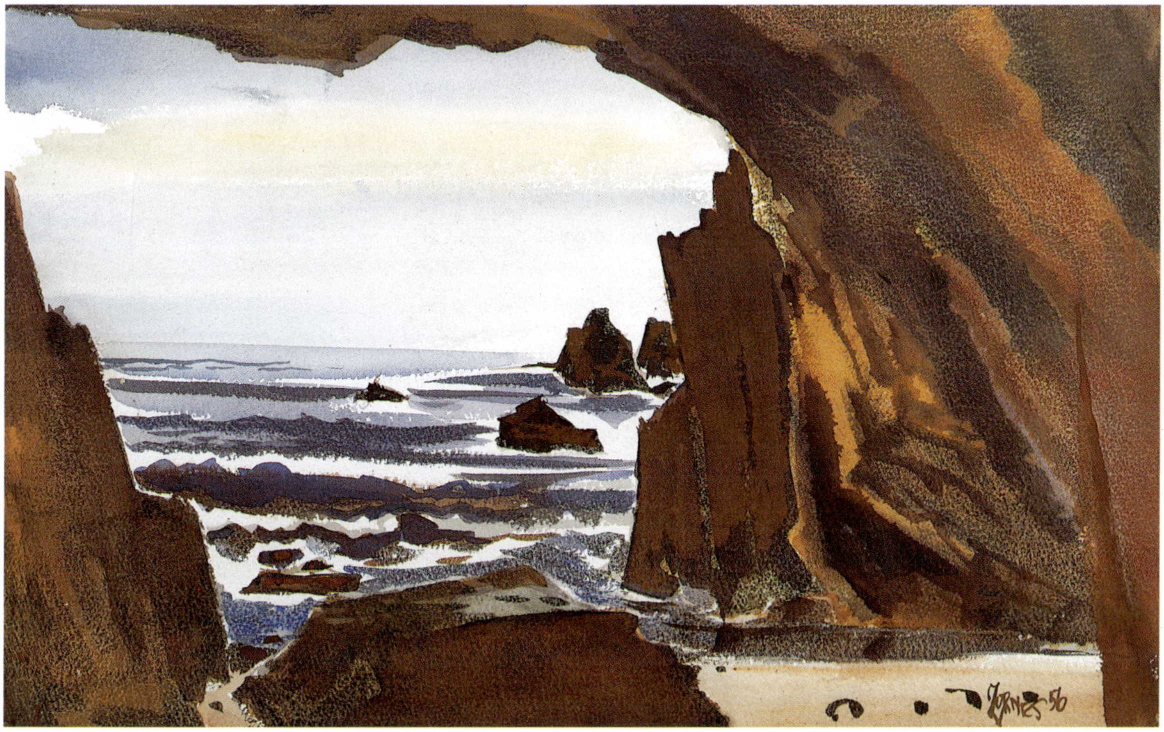

Sea Cave. 1956 Watercolor 13 x 22 in. Private Collection.

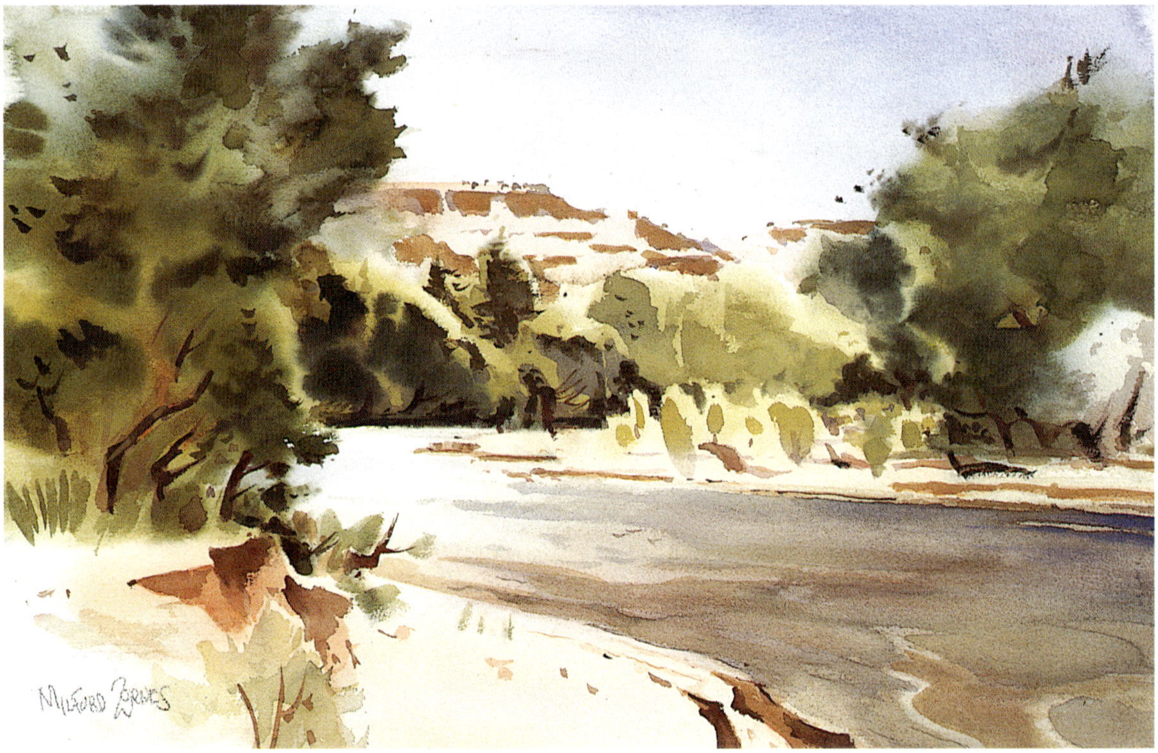

The East Fork. 1958 Watercolor 15 x 22 in. Courtesy Barbara Beretich.

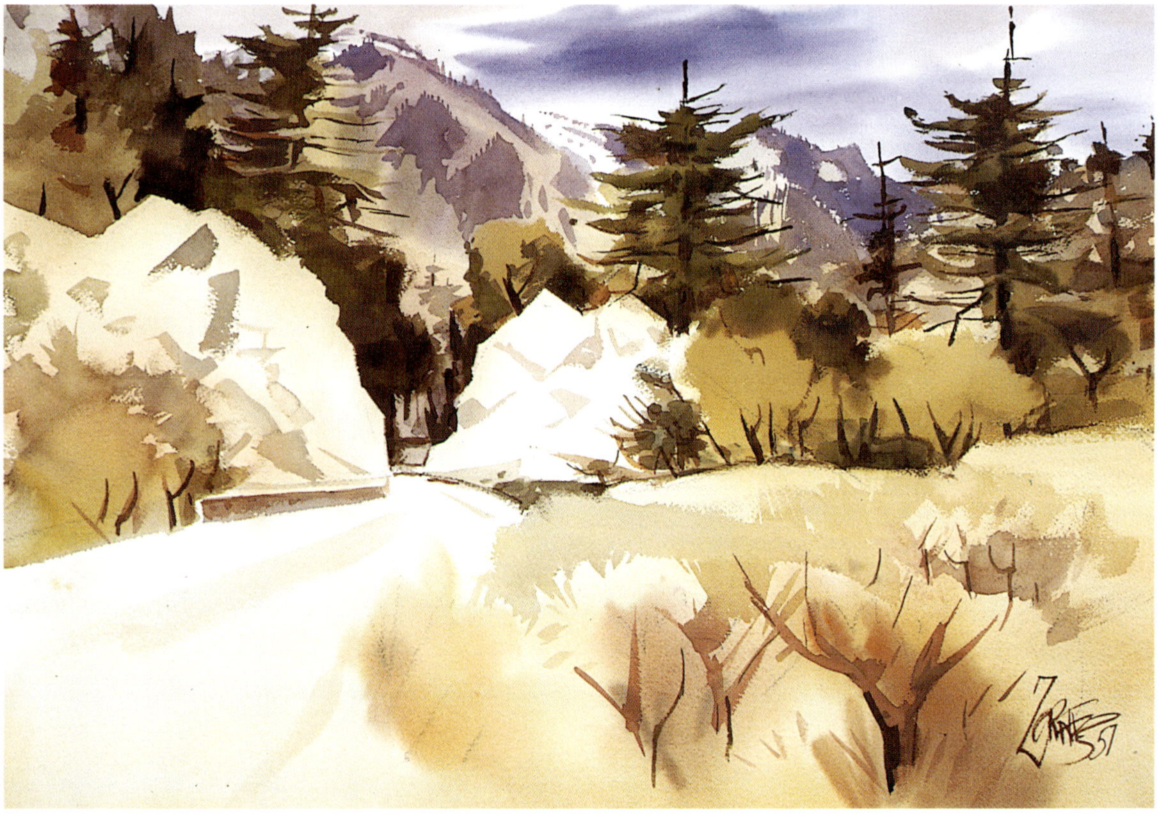

Road to Mt. Baldy. 1957 Watercolor 20 x 28 in.

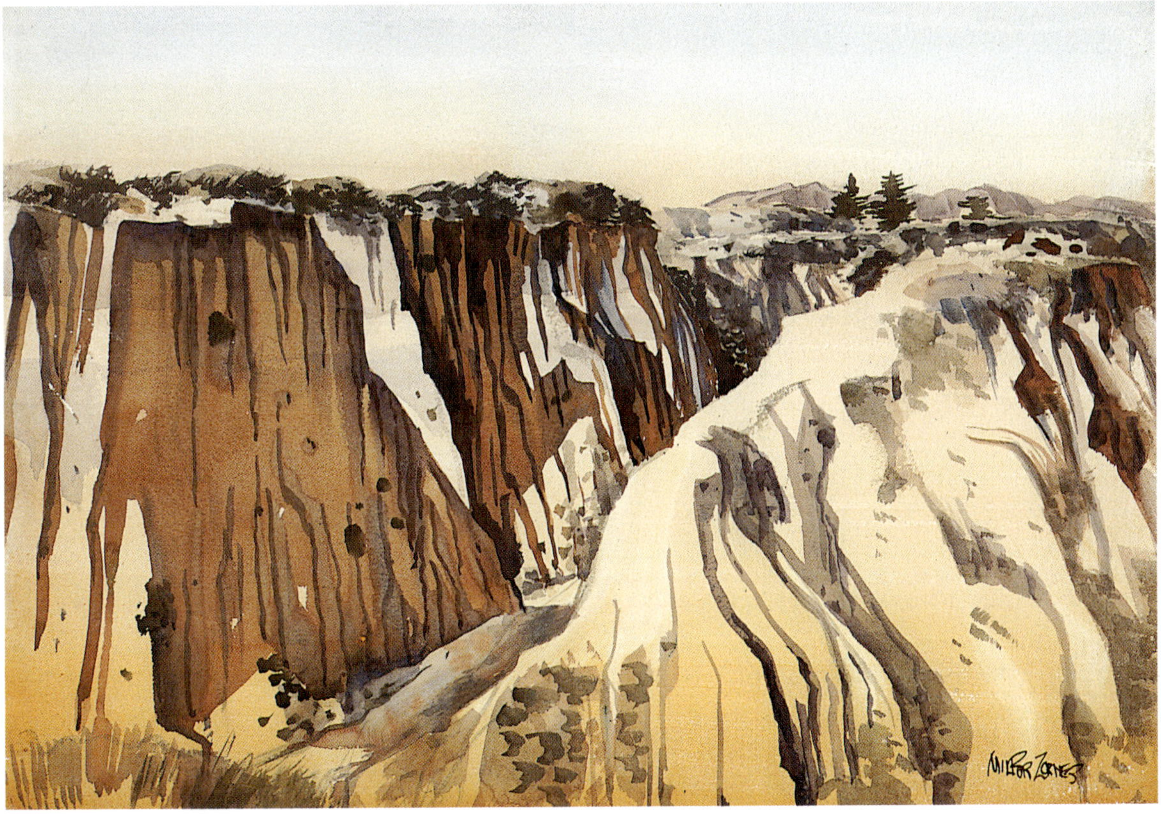

Barrouks de San Clemente. 1958 Watercolor 22 x 38 in.

During this era many artists, art collectors, museum curators and art critics were most interested in abstract or non-objective art. As a part of his natural development Zornes was interested in strong abstract designs in each of his works, but found the concept of abandoning subject matter altogether unappealing. Since the 1940s he had been working to eliminate detail in his works and focus on large, colorful shapes and patterns, but this was a difficult process and took him a number of years to perfect. Often he started paintings as a bold, simple statement, but ultimately they came out looking very different according to how much rendering and detail he applied in addition to the basic visual statement. Zornes commented: "This matter of when to stop painting or should I say of determining when the painting is finished, is a very tricky matter. I've overworked more paintings than I care to admit, but this is the only way one learns."

The late 1950s and early 1960s was a strenuous period for Zornes. Artistically he was pushing himself to strengthen, simplify and resolve his approach to watercolor painting. He spent much of his time painting, drawing and seeking out landscape locations that provided interesting possibilities for bold compositional statements. This concentrated involvment left little time for selling art or working, so financial difficulties soon followed. His situation began to resolve by 1962.

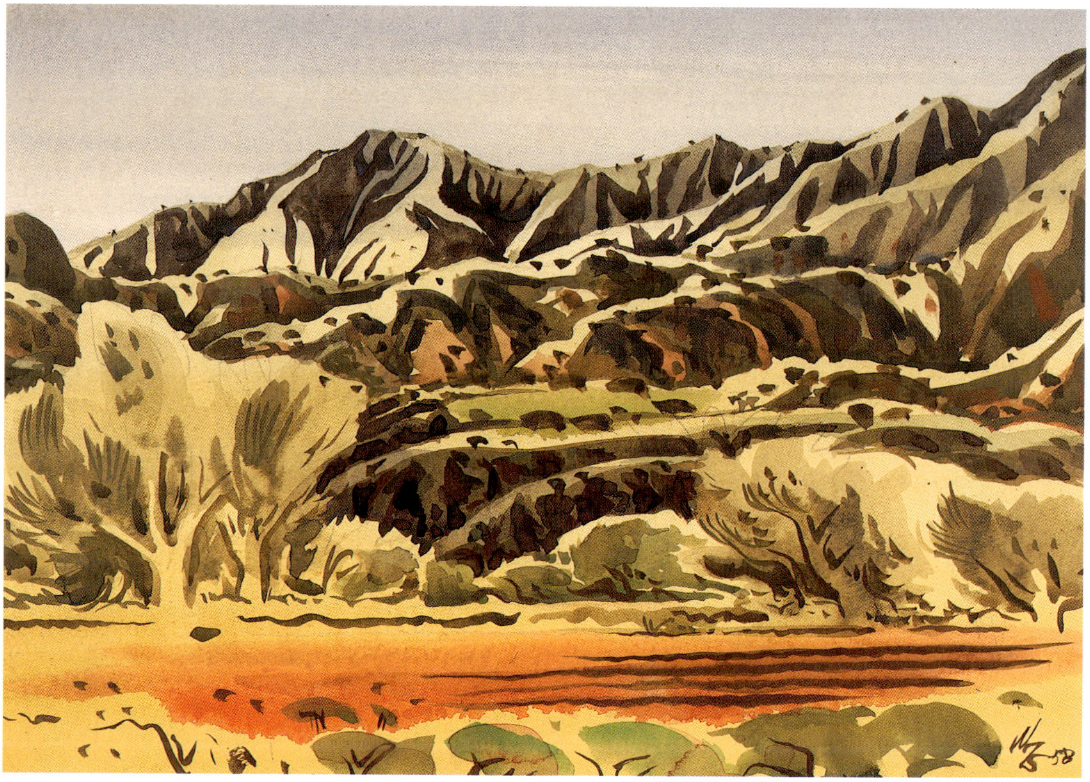

Desert Valley. 1958 Watercolor 22 x 30 in.

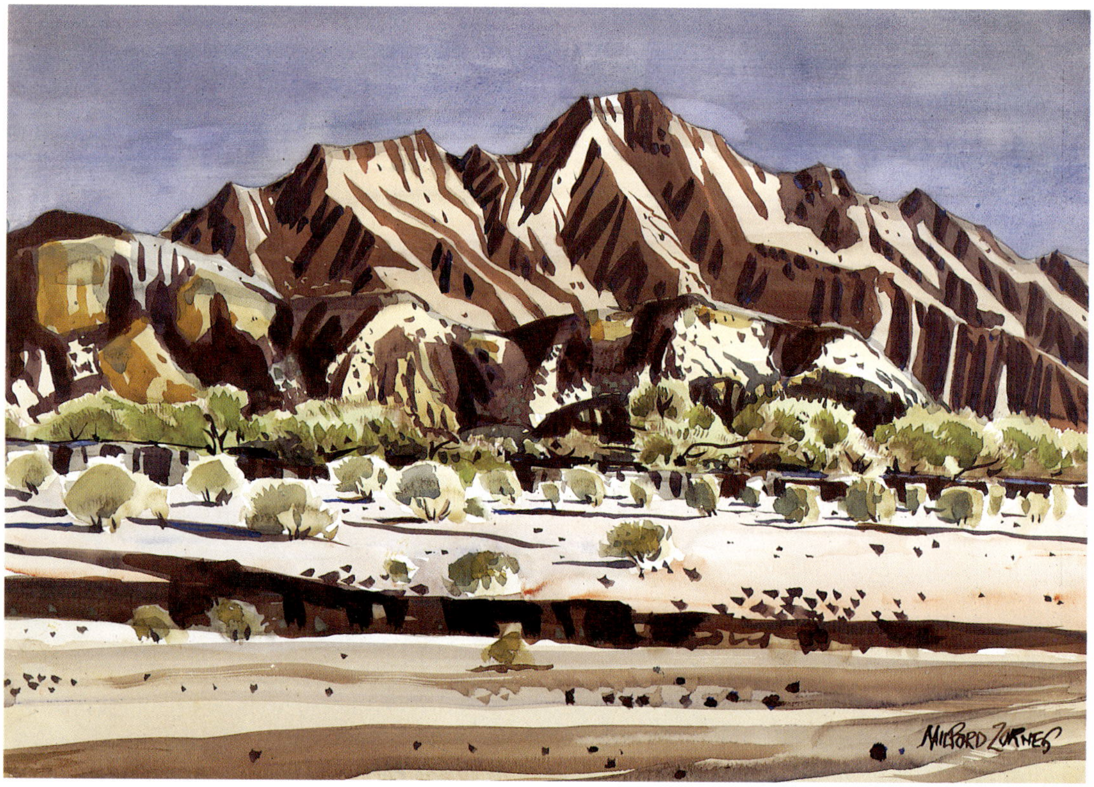

Simi Valley. 1959 Watercolor 12 x 17 in. Private Collection.

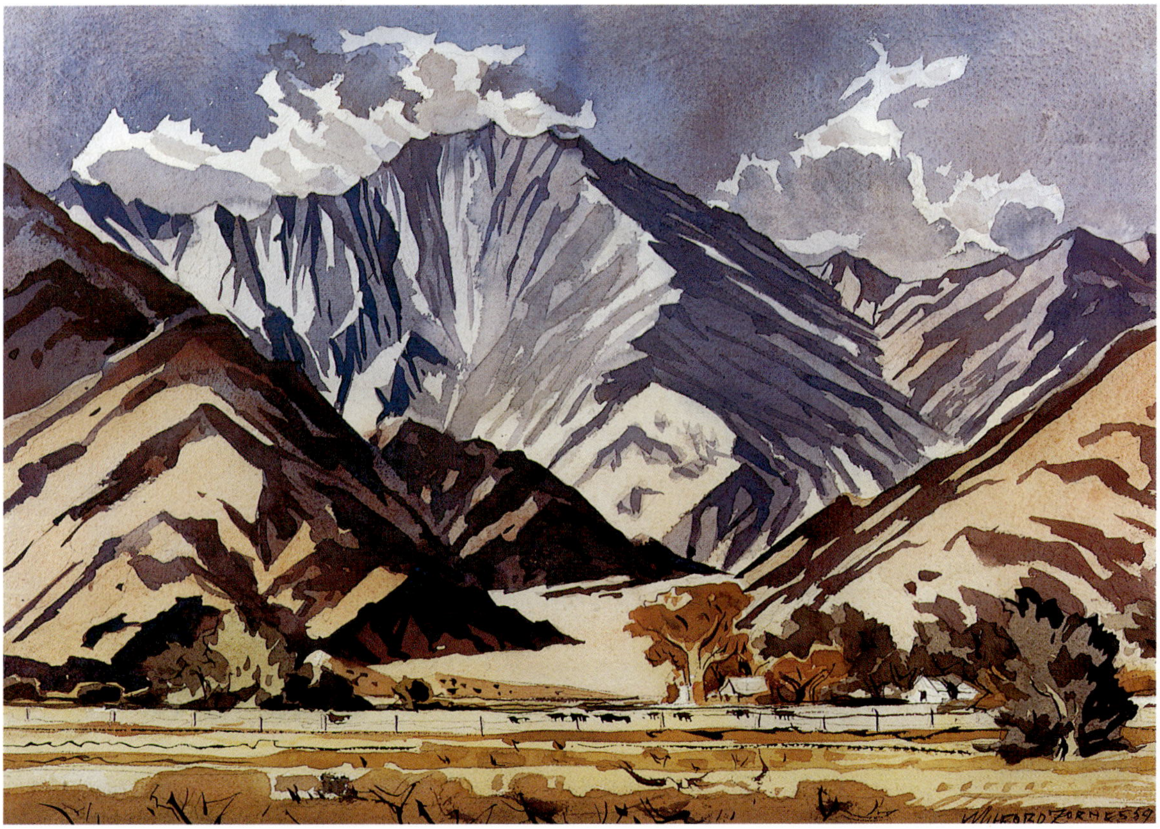

Mt. San Jacinto. 1959 Watercolor 21 x 29 in. Donna and Robert Ortleib Collection.

A key event was the advent of watercolor workshop classes sponsored by regional art associations. Zornes was hired on a regular basis to travel from city to city throughout the southwestern states giving talks, painting demonstrations and exhibiting his art. Newspaper and magazine reporters wrote about his shows wherever he went. This grass roots approach helped build a general interest in watercolor painting and introduced his art to a new audience.

Nationally Zornes was also receiving some noteworthy recognition. His watercolor titled "Beach Party" received a Medal of Honor from the American Watercolor Society Annual Exhibition in New York City. Members of the prestigious National Academy of Design, also in New York, elected him as associate of their organization. *American Artist* magazine followed with a feature article, written by Zornes and accompanied by reproductions of his recent paintings.

In retrospect, it is clear that the twenty years following World War II was a difficult period for Zornes as he adjusted to the post-war economy, social changes and shift in public attitudes about art. In spite of these problems, Zornes continued to develop his style of watercolor painting and by the early 1960s was once again receiving national acclaim.

4

Since 1963

"I enjoy pictures that say what they have to say, simply, directly and seemingly with little labored effort. I am happy with my own paintings only when I give little thought to the actual application of paint to paper. It is only the truth of the subject matter and integrity of design that matters."

—M.Z.

In 1963 Zornes took a break from his work schedule to ride along with a friend who was picking up a new automobile in Detroit. While leisurely cruising back to the West Coast they decided to stop in Utah to visit Edith Hamlin Dixon. When they arrived at this scenic spot on the edge of Zion National Park they found that the property, log cabin and art studio, built by Maynard Dixon was for sale. Zornes purchased it and within the year moved his family there.

His wife Pat, an animal and nature lover, was delighted with this move. She agreed to set up and operate a watercolor workshop class in the large studio adjacent to their home. For twelve years Zornes offered painting instruction to students who would spend one or two weeks at local motels. Each day they would paint on location near the school or in Zion National Park. Although many of these classes were attended by small numbers of students, the quality of education was considered high enough that they could receive college credit through Brigham Young University in Provo, Utah.

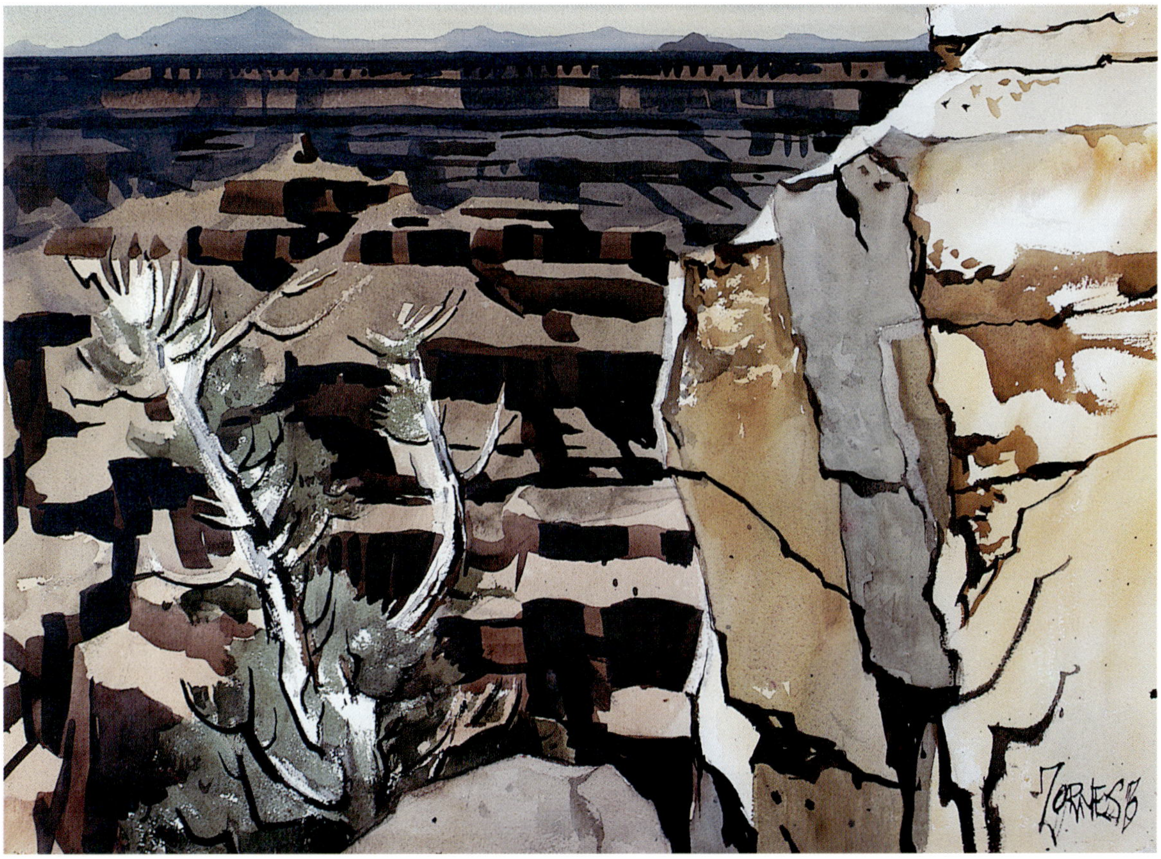

From the North Rim. 1976 Watercolor 22 x 30 in. Clark Family Collection.

As Zornes continued to win important awards and write articles about painting, the publicity he received opened many doors. Watercolor societies all over America invited him to visit and give teaching/demonstration programs. In California he set up workshops for artists to paint on location and then gather for a critique at the day's end. Each summer he offered these classes in Laguna Beach and Riverside.

While teaching art had always been part of Zornes' career it was becoming increasingly important to him. He wrote: "It is my opinion that art is communication and the artist can if he is talented as a teacher and believes in the language of art find it stimulating and worthwhile to teach in conjunction with his own efforts as a painter. Teaching is, after all, a selfish exercise if it is to have vitality and the artist can grow in his thought and production through the formulating of his knowledge to benefit others.

I do not teach people to paint pictures. I try to teach them to think as painters, to find their own uniqueness in ways of seeing and to demand of themselves skills and techniques and the need to understand structure and design. With all those who study with me, I take a simple attitude that if I can be responsible for anyone seeing more in the world around

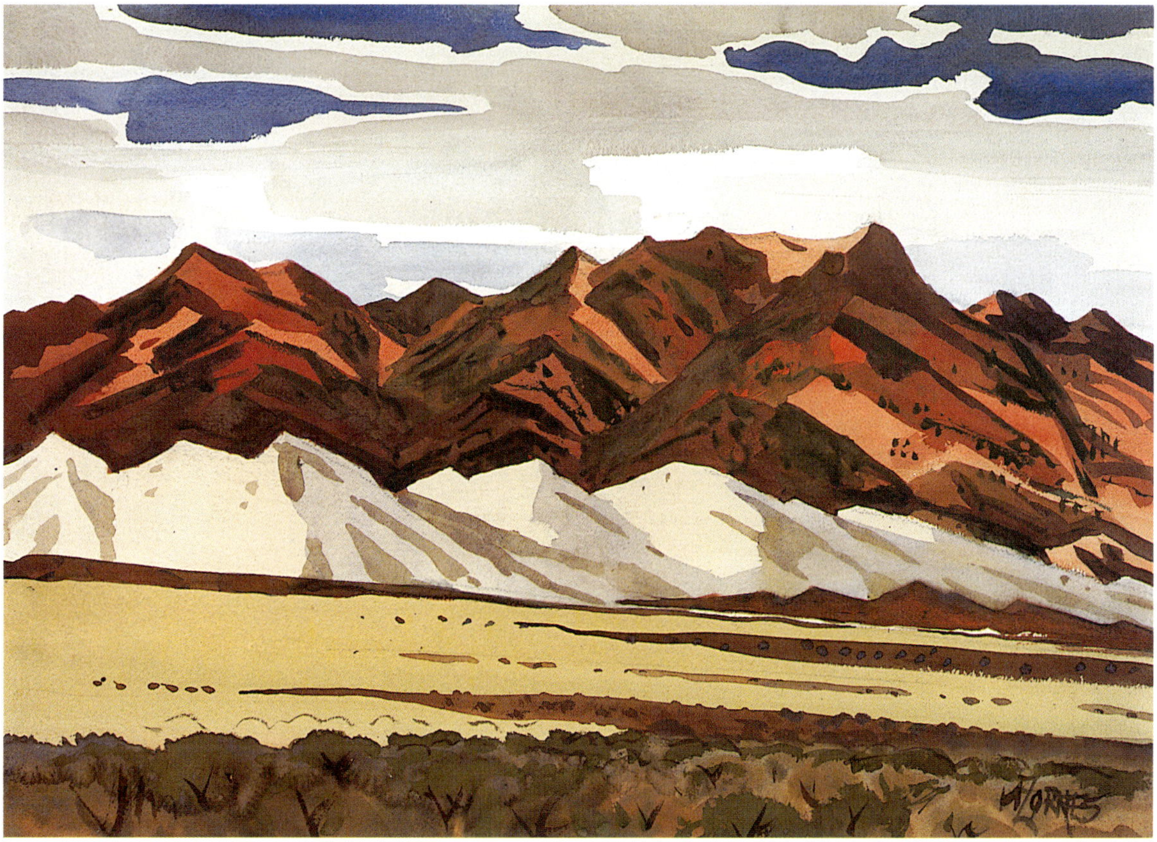

Desert Patterns. Watercolor 22 x 30 in.

them and through observation and thought being able to give form and meaning to their seeing, then I am earning my salt, so to speak, because I am enabling them to enrich their lives.''

By the late 1960s these teaching opportunities expanded into international travel workshop classes arranged by privately owned organizations. Therman Huett and Tony Van Hasselt set up two of the most prominent companies offering study programs in foreign countries. These classes were taught by Zornes, Dong Kingman, George Post and other highly respected artist/teachers. While teaching these classes Zornes was able to paint on location in Hawaii and many foreign countries including Spain, Puerto Rico, Mexico and Ireland.

These workshops did not always provide the best circumstances to pursue new areas of artistic interest, but they did provide an opportunity for travel. As Zornes expressed it: ''Travel is important to me. Perhaps painting, for me, has been an excuse to travel. I am fully aware that an artist could find a world of discovery and not move from his studio or his immediate surroundings and I have often envied those who have the resources within themselves to do this. For me, going beyond geographical horizons is a way to get beyond my mental horizons as well, so that travel can be

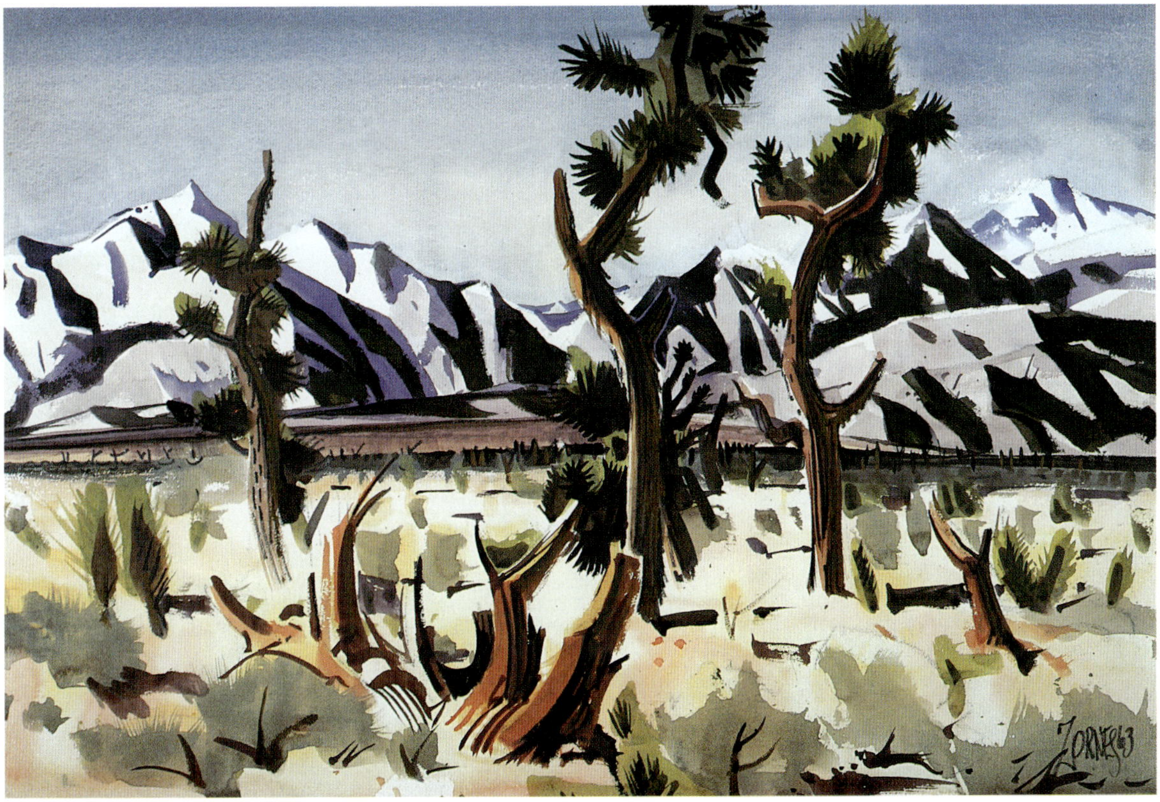

Mojave Landscape. 1963 Watercolor 21 x 30 in.

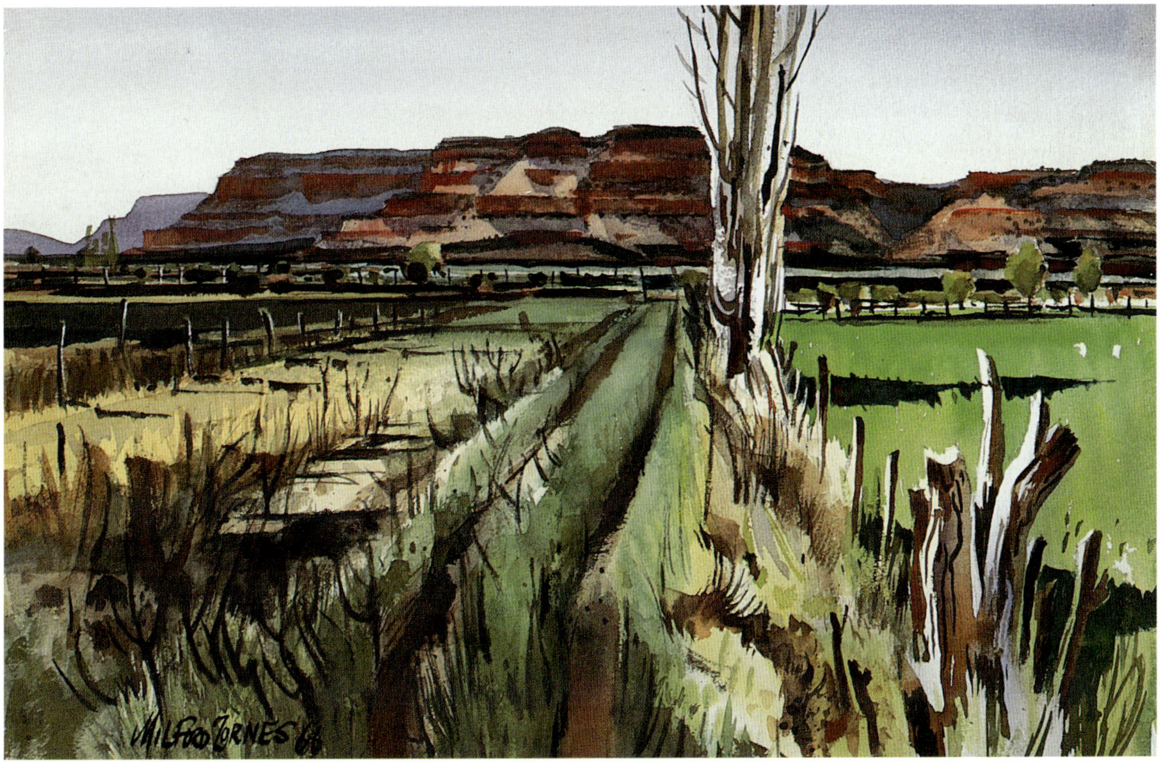

Spring in the Valley. 1966 Watercolor 20 x 29 in.

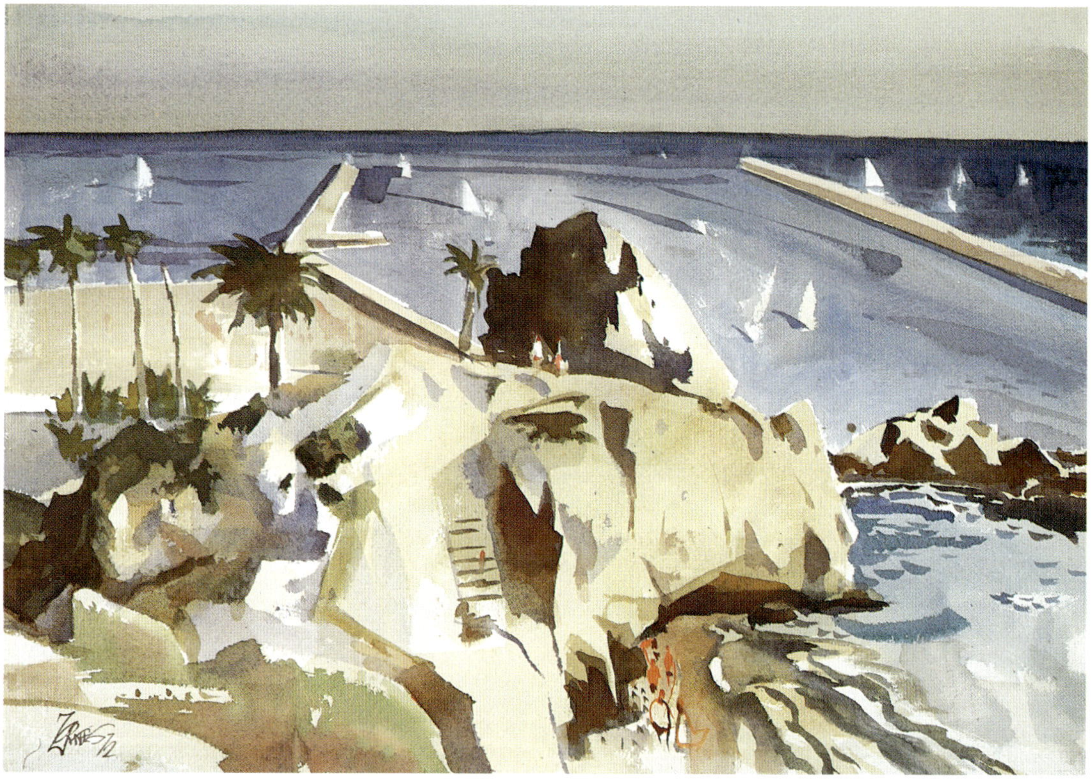

Corona del Mar. 1972 Watercolor 22 x 30 in.

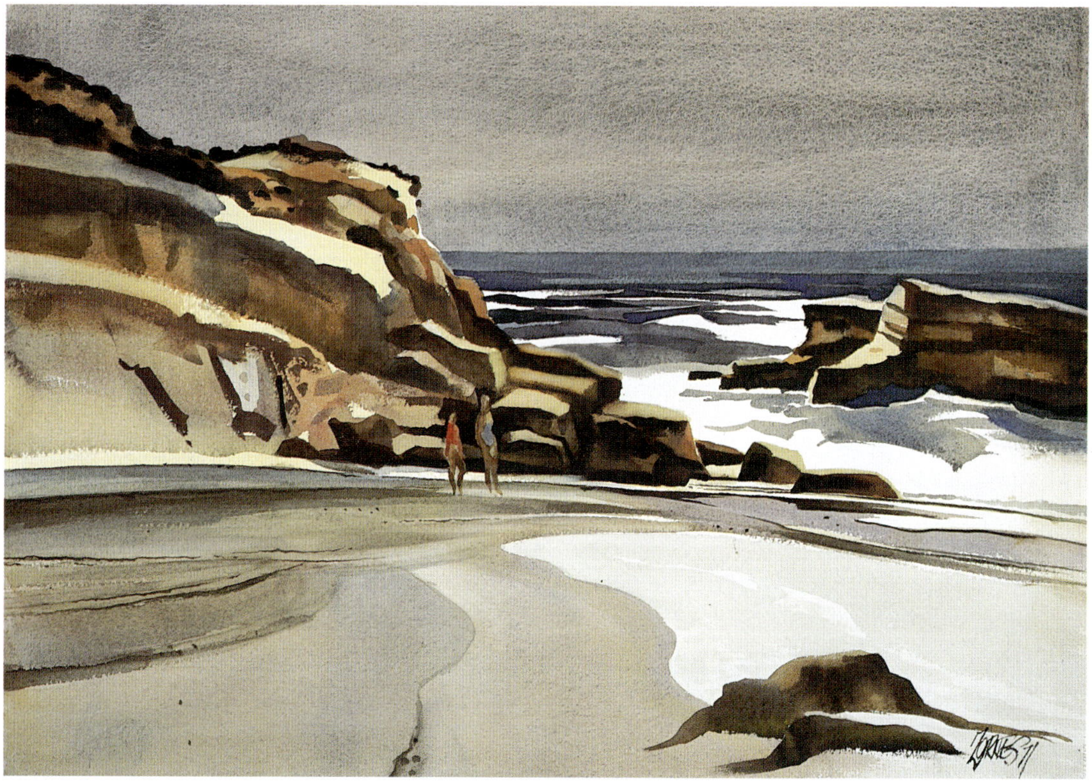

Diver's Cove. 1971 Watercolor 22 x 30 in. Courtesy Barbara Beretich.

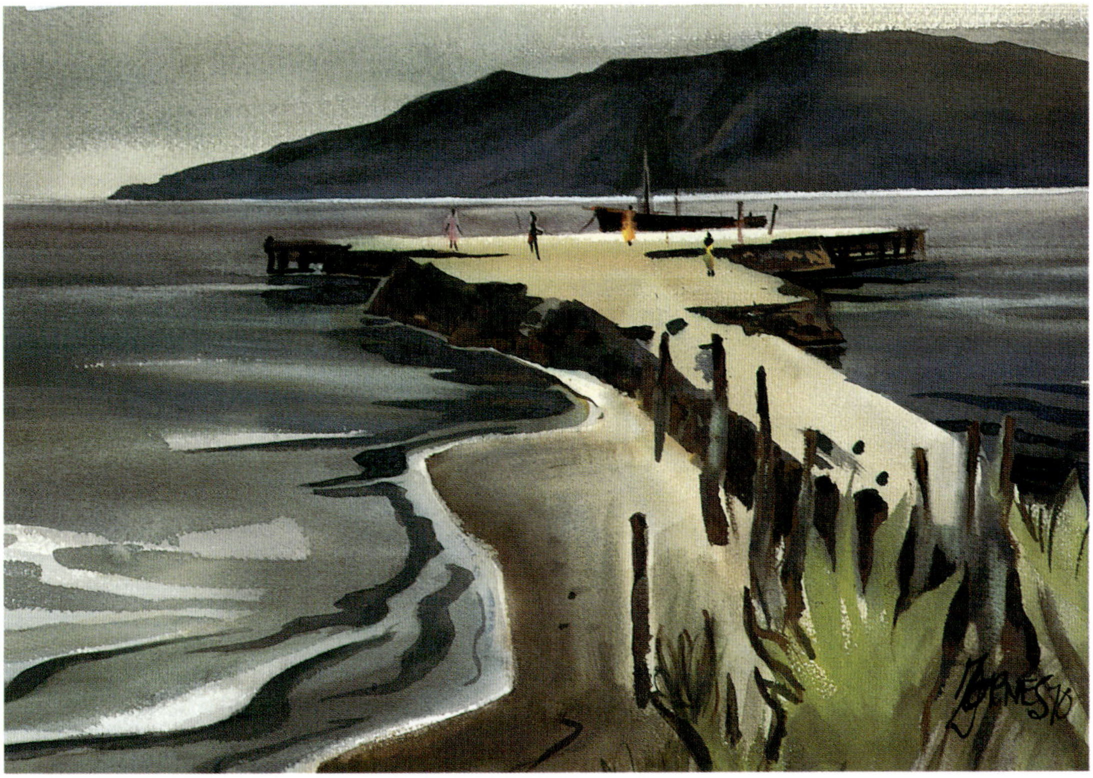

Molakai. 1970 Watercolor 15 x 22 in.

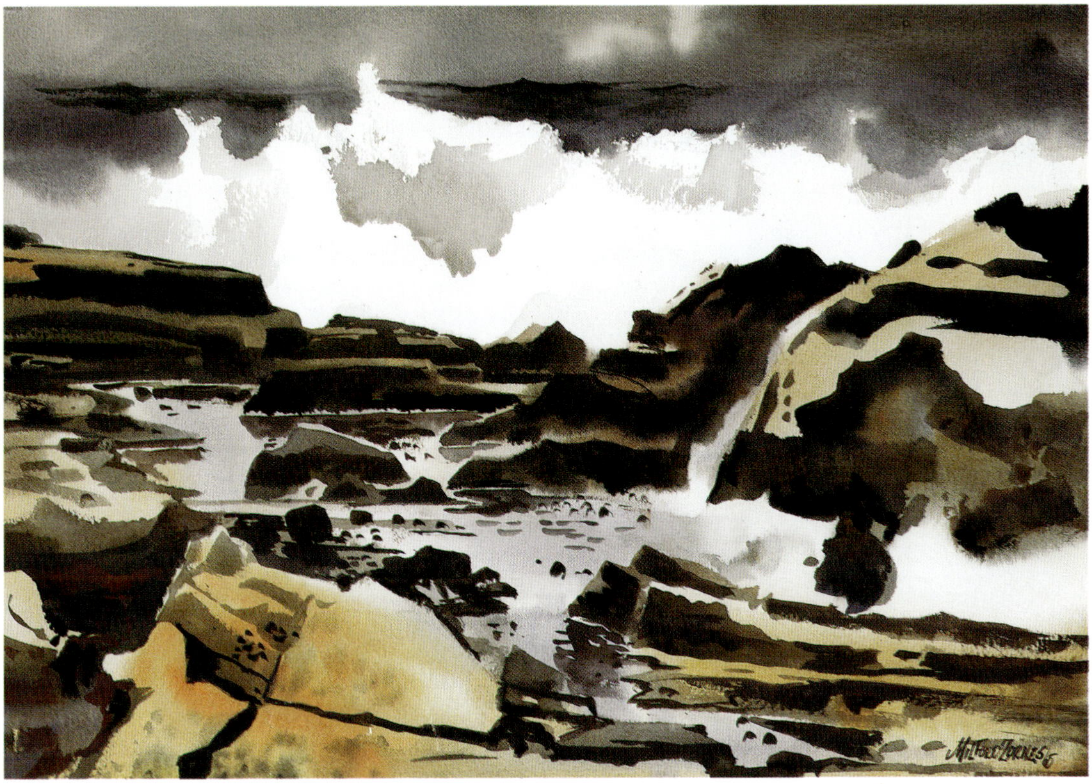

Breaking Sea. 1965 Watercolor 22 x 30 in. J.B. Ruffin Collection.

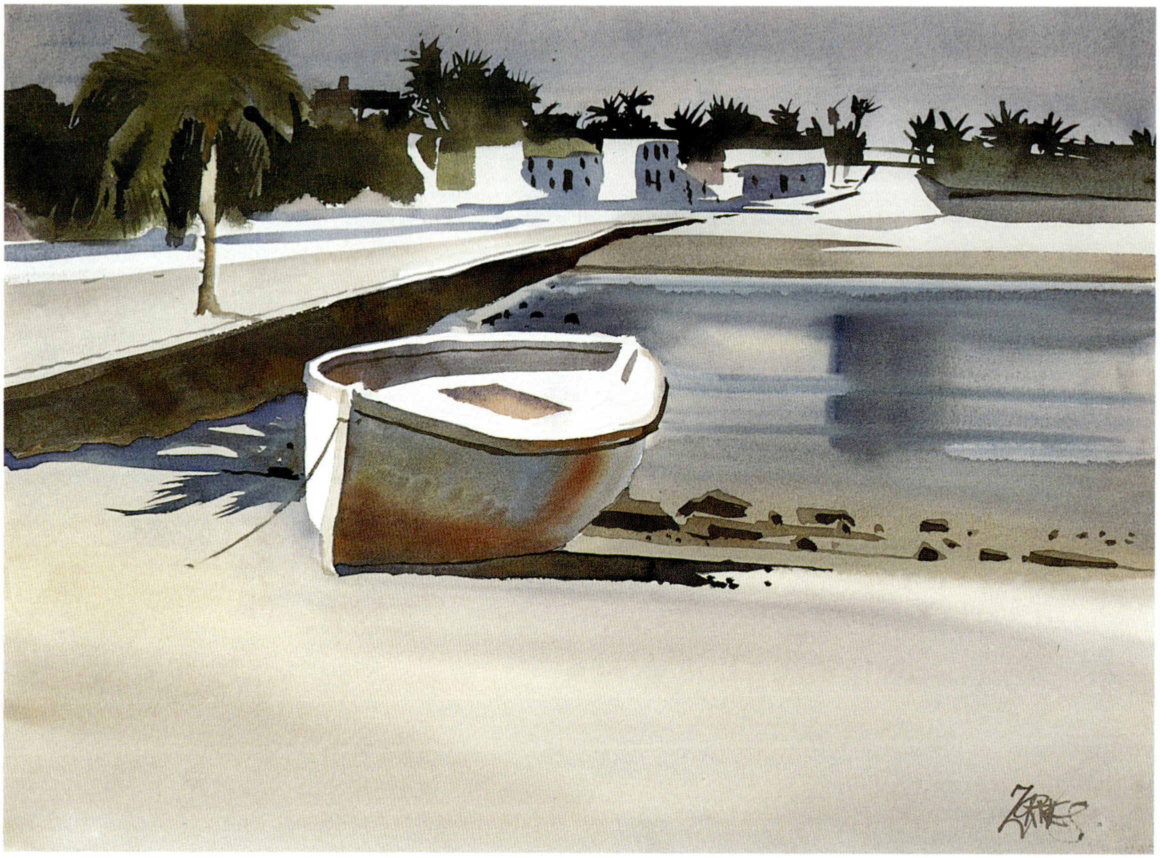

La Paz. 1975 Watercolor 22 x 30 in.

a way to nourish whatever creative effort I have. It brings exterior kinds of adventures and exotic experiences which in themselves offer sufficient pictorial material. I need only exert drafting, painting and design skills to claim expression through them.

Every traveler sees and discovers according to whatever he tries to see and what he wants to discover. As a painter I seldom ponder the political, social and economic concerns of the countries I visit. Mine is a visual acquaintance. In the natural and man made forms are written for me what I need to know of the history, the natural forces and circumstances that shape the character of lands and people.''

Once Zornes established an international teaching reputation many more offers came his way. In the early 1970s Lunda Hoyle Gill, one of his former students set up several teaching/lecture programs in conjunction with the Oklahoma Museum of Art. While in Oklahoma he was introduced to Dr. Richard Hancock from the University of Oklahoma. Through this contact Zornes was hired to teach several weeks each year at the University's cultural retreat, Hacienda El Cobano in Colima, Mexico. It is located on Mexico's tropical West Coast, an ideal setting for painting and teaching. Within an hour he could take students to traditional moun-

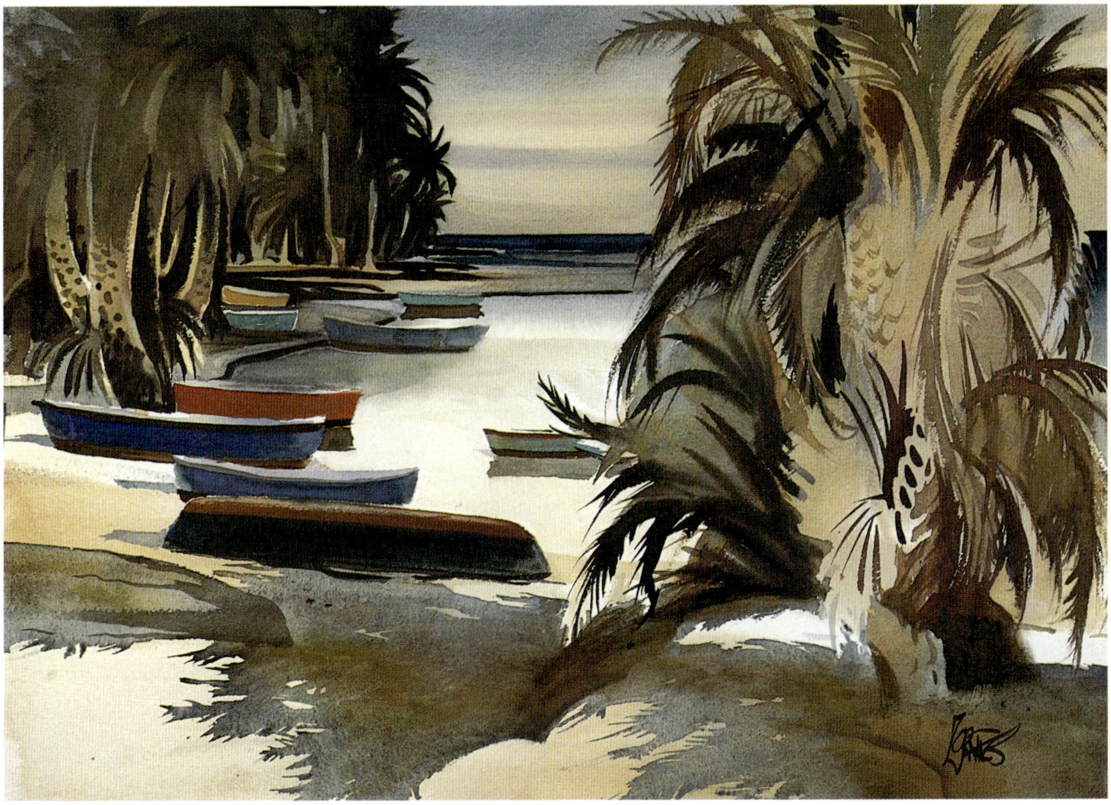

May in La Paz. 1975 Watercolor 22 x 30 in.

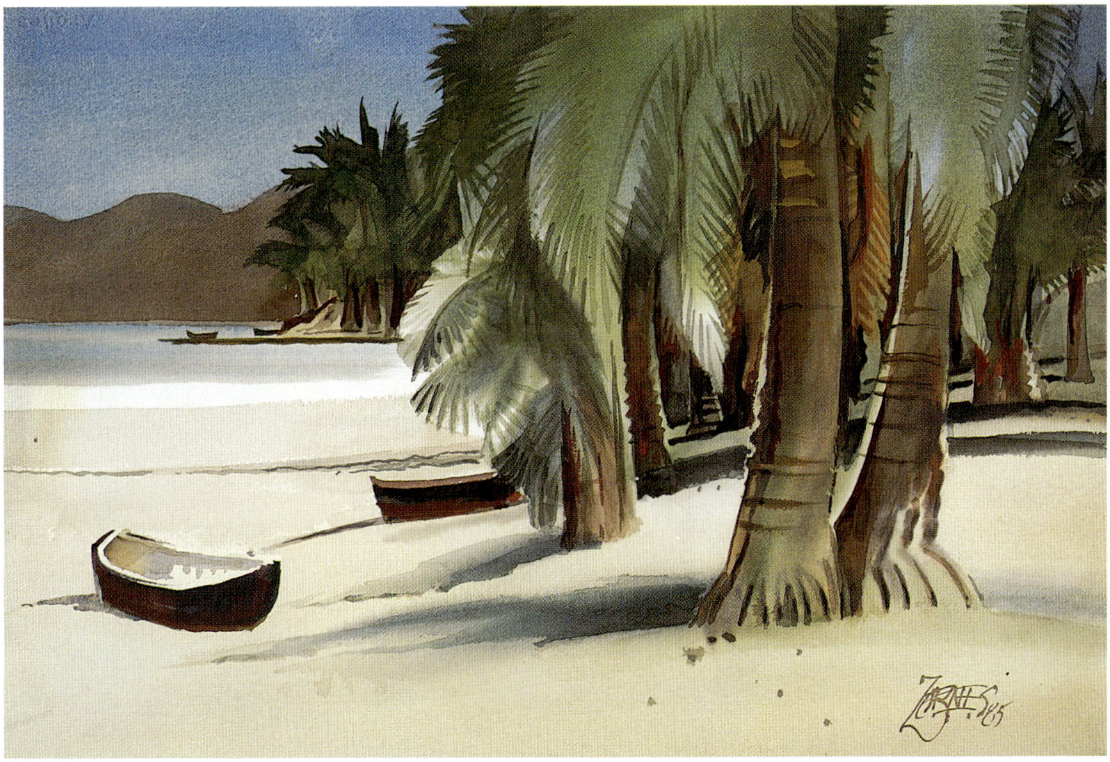

Baja Shore. 1973 Watercolor 22 x 30 in.

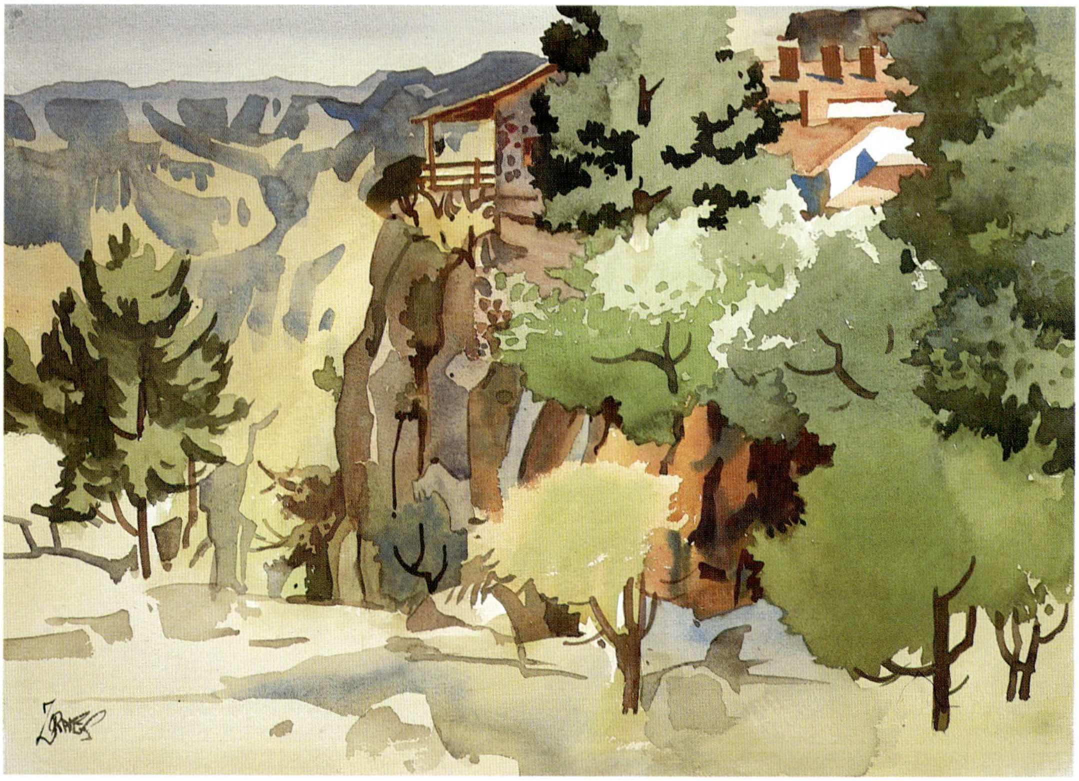

Pasada Divisadera. 1976 Watercolor 22 x 30 in. Courtesy David Howard Fine Art.

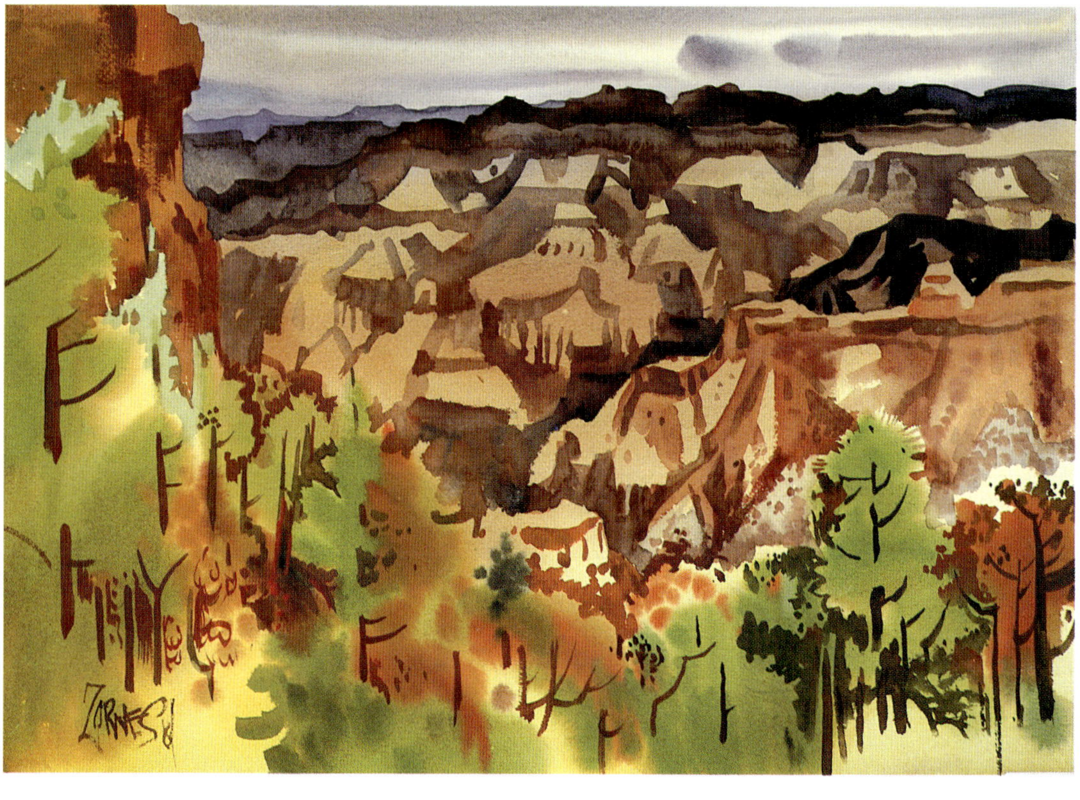

Barranka De Cobre. 1976 Watercolor 22 x 30 in.

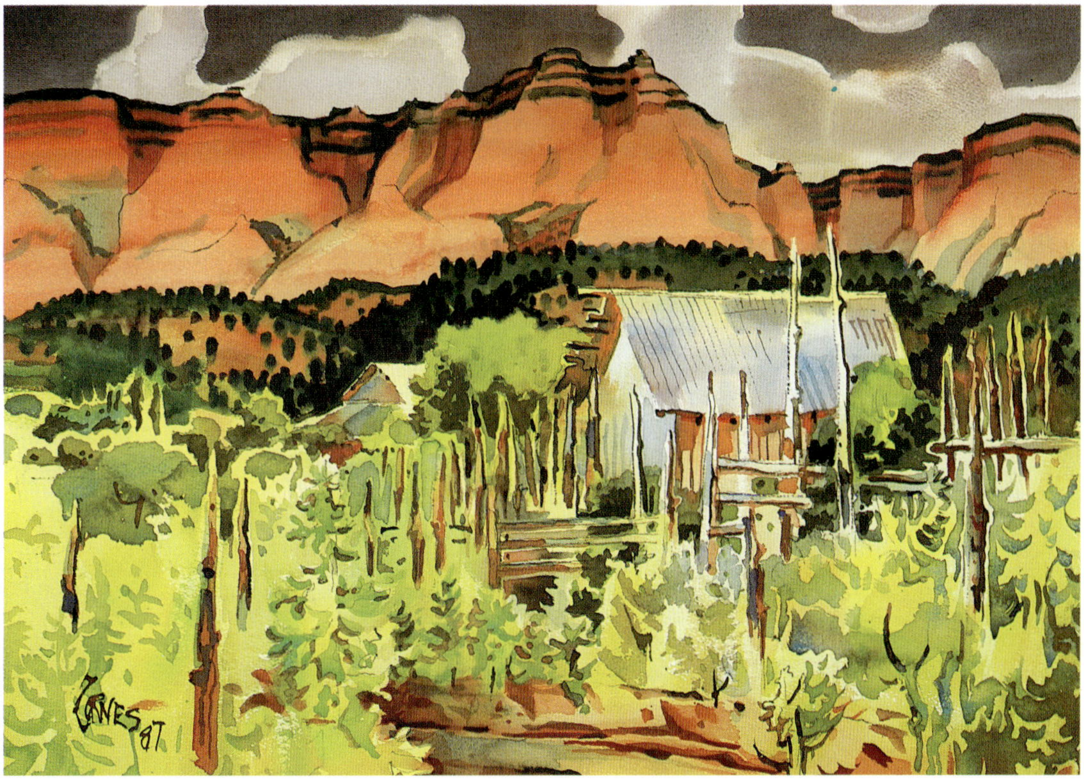

Ranch in the Valley. 1987 Watercolor 22 x 30 in.

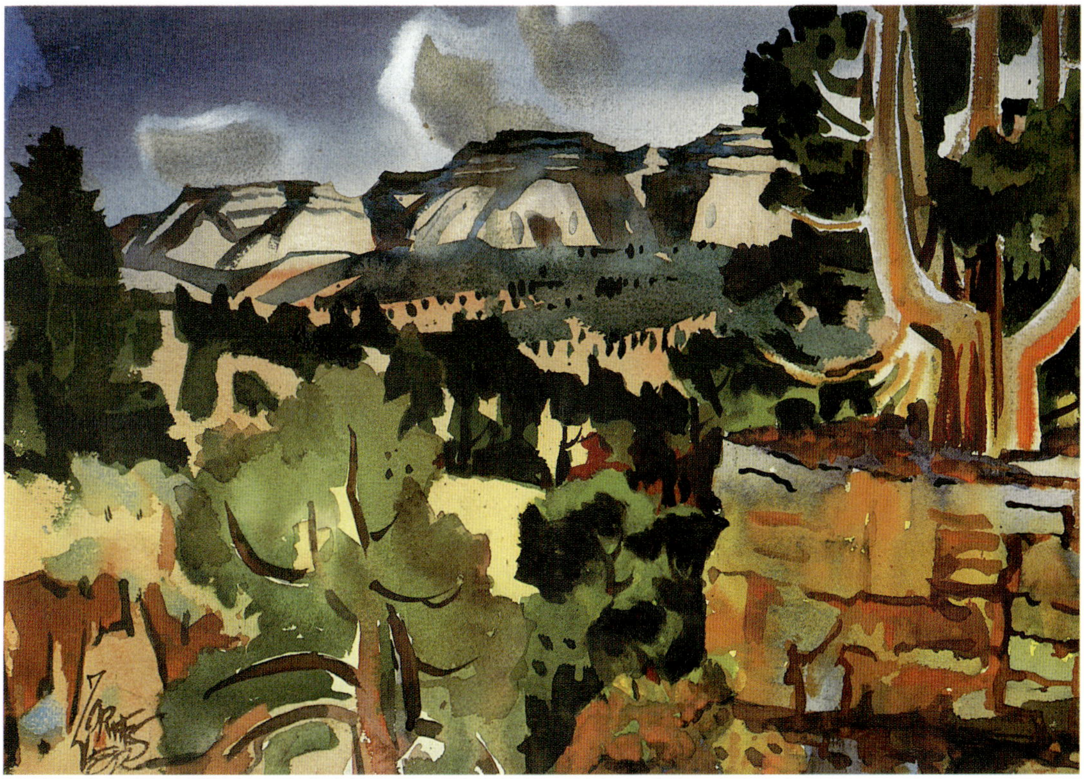

Carmel Mesas. 1980 Watercolor 22 x 30 in. The Leichtling Collection.

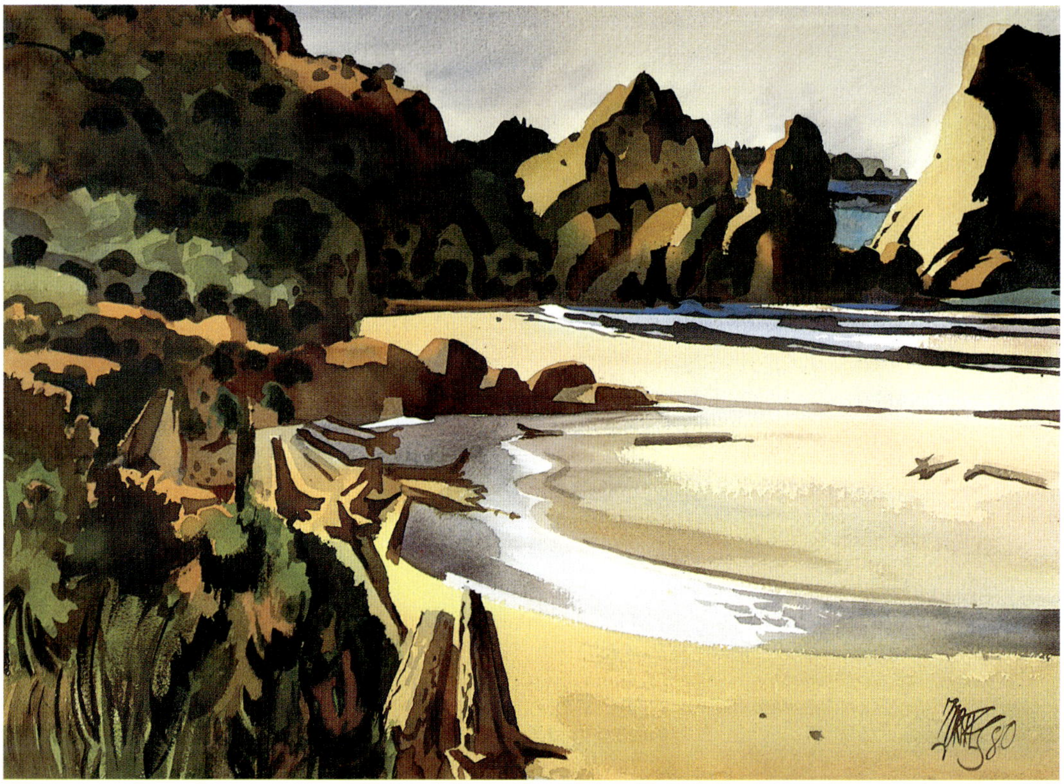

Sea Shore Sentinals. 1980 Watercolor 23 x 34 in. Harvey A. Reifsnyder Collection.

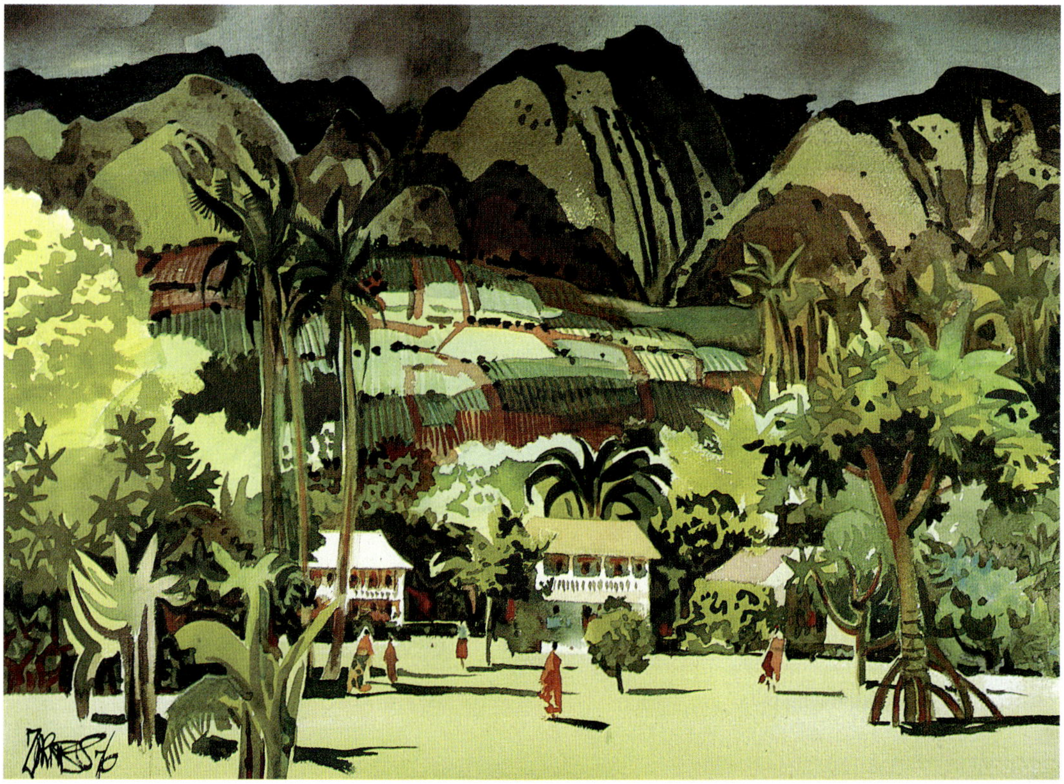

Up from Lahaina. 1976 Watercolor 22 x 30 in. Mr. and Mrs. Jerry Juergens Collection.

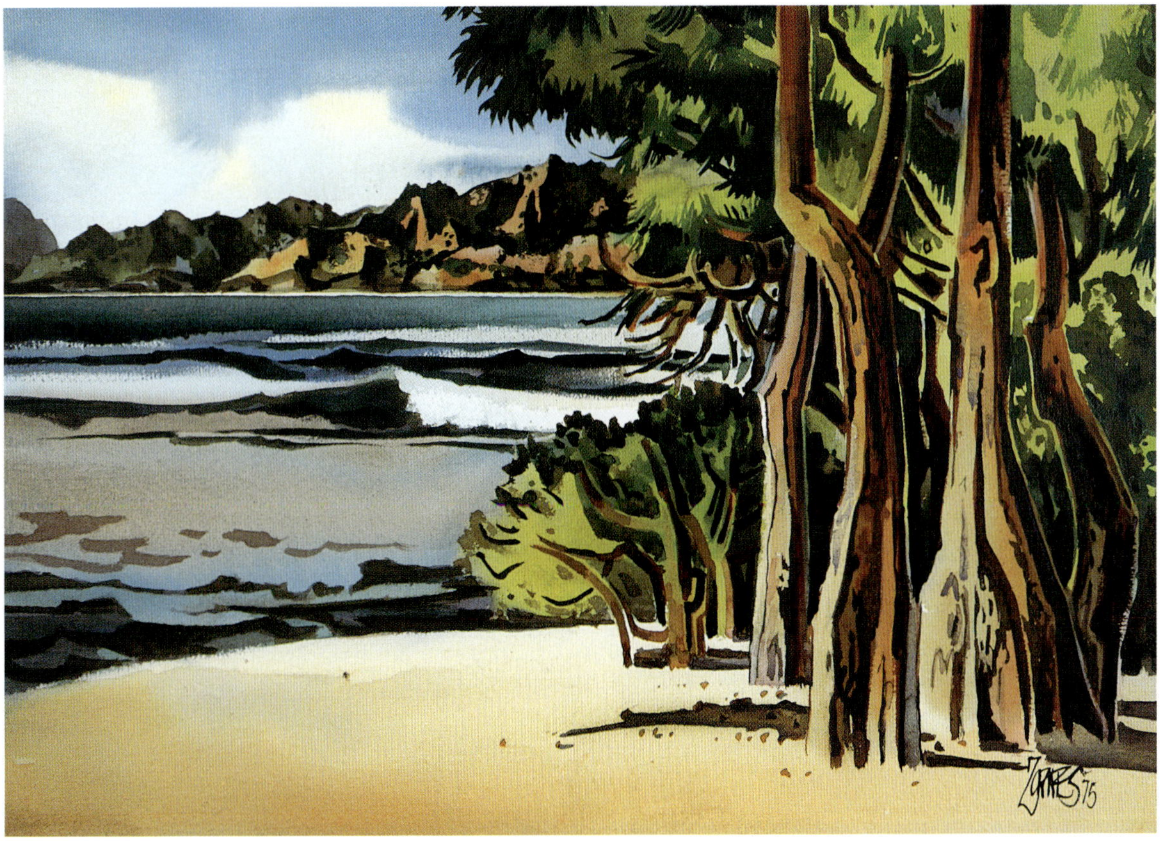

The Sea at Kapaa. 1975 Watercolor 22 x 30 in. Mr. and Mrs. Jerry Juergens Collection.

tain villages, open areas in clear view of a great volcano, or to the commercial seaport of Manzanillo. Often Zornes would stay in Mexico for extended periods of time and has produced hundreds of watercolors depicting this country.

Dr. Hancock was also the president of V.O.O.M. a missionary division of the Protestant Episcopal Church of the United States. After visiting Bluefields on Nicaragua's Atlantic coast Hancock came up with the idea of having V.O.O.M. subsidize a painting excursion for Zornes. In 1974 he traveled to Managua, Bluefields and Corn Island. A selection of the paintings Zornes produced, along with his writings about the excursion, was published in a 1977 book titled *A Journey To Nicaragua*. Although he is not a member of this church, Zornes felt V.O.O.M. was sincerely helping the people of Nicaragua and agreed to donate all proceeds from the sales of the paintings to their missionary endeavors.

Since the 1970s Zornes has accepted many teaching offers and has continued to travel, often combining the two. He has visited South and Central America, Africa, Indonesia, China and Europe as well as taught classes in nineteen states. On each of his trips he has completed several watercolors, generally his teaching demonstration paintings.

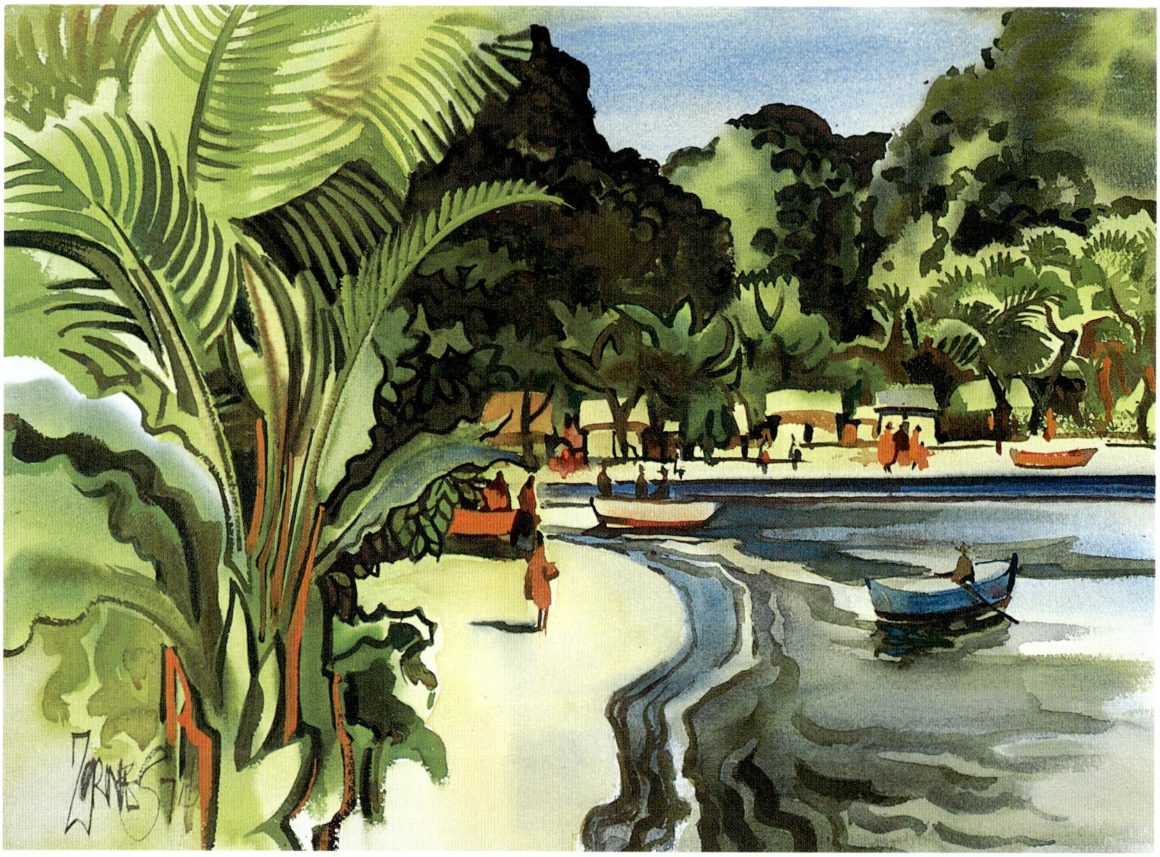

Yalapa Shores. 1973 Watercolor 22 x 30 in. Courtesy Barbara Beretich.

When not teaching Zornes often paints on location or finishes works in his studio. He and his wife Pat live in homes they have established in Utah and Southern California and many of his recent works were inspired by the landscape in those regions.

Whenever Zornes produces a painting, be it in a foreign country or his back yard, he generally follows a series of procedures. He notes: "When I go into a remote valley and see a home nestled into some trees by a river or visit a harbor where ships are docked and ocean breezes blow, I often become inspired to paint. But when I begin to work I pay little attention to the immediate emotional attraction of the scene and focus on what is in front of me as a design problem.

Once the basic composition is established I consider color, if it's a bright sunny day the colors will be weak on the surfaces where light is striking and rich in the shadows. If it's an overcast day the lighting is even and colorful throughout. In the early morning or late afternoon a warm glow often bathes the environment and the shadows become opaque.

The next major consideration is how to create the illusion of three dimensional forms on a flat surface, while maintaining the strength of my overall composition. Here the key word is contrast. A readable pattern

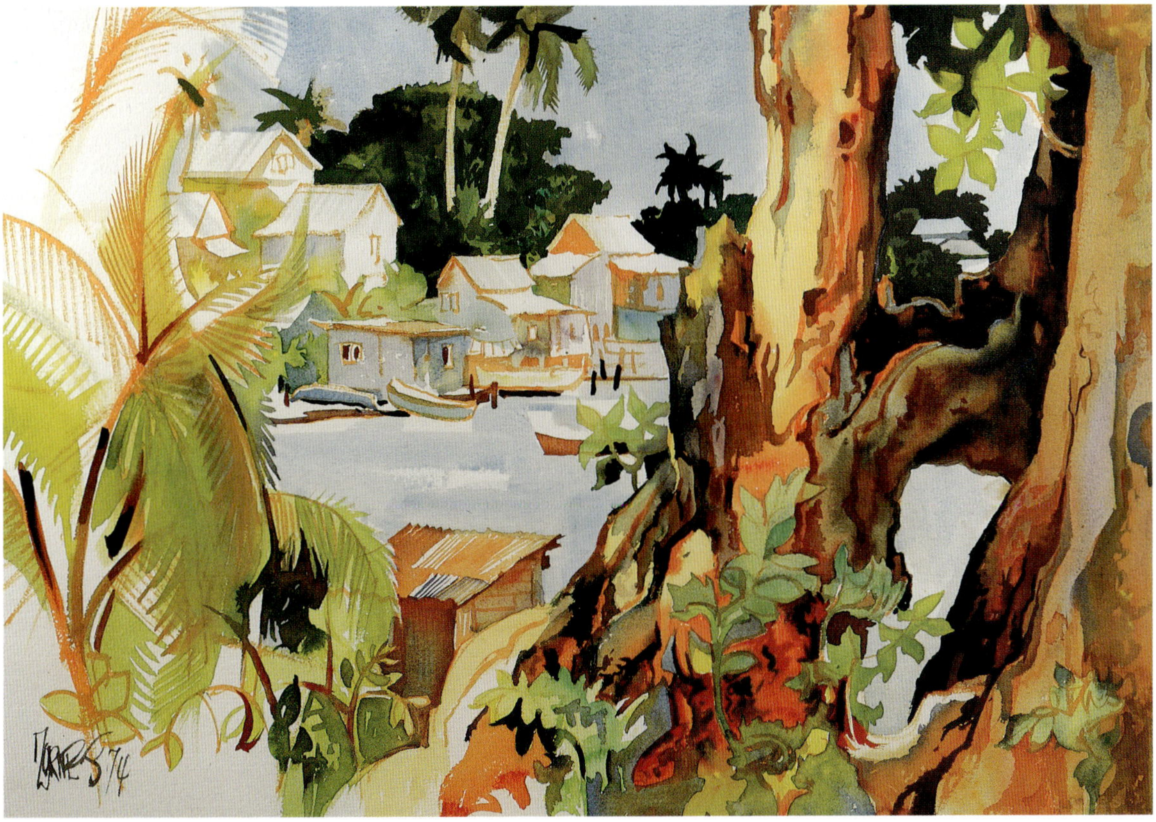

Beholding Harbor. 1974 Watercolor 22 x 30 in. Donna and Robert Ortleib Collection.

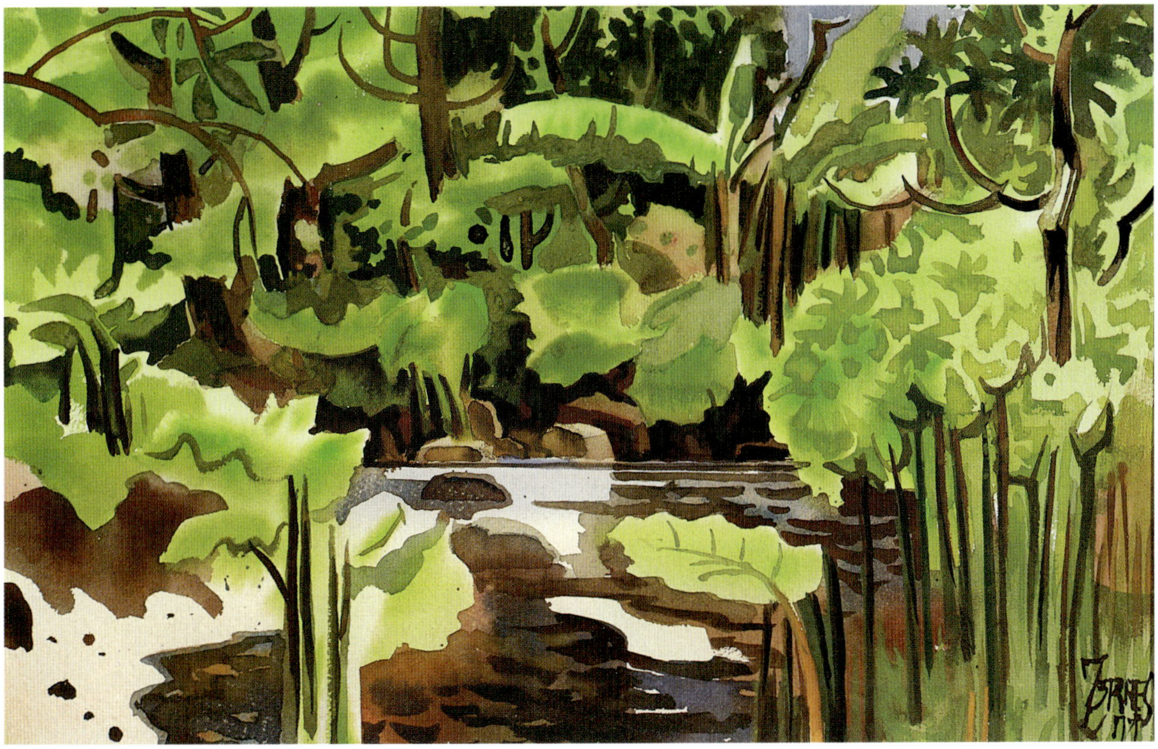

Arroyo Cobano. 1977 Watercolor 15 x 22 in.

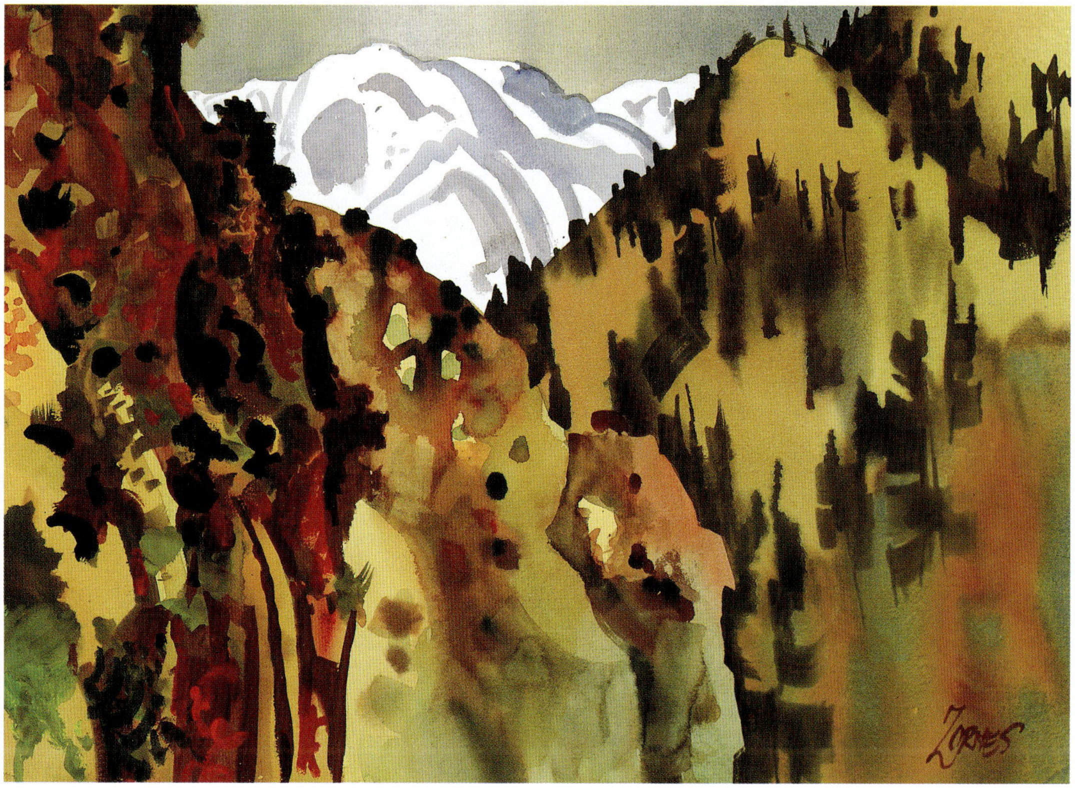

San Antonio Canyon. Watercolor 22 x 30 in. Bob and Toni Crisell Collection.

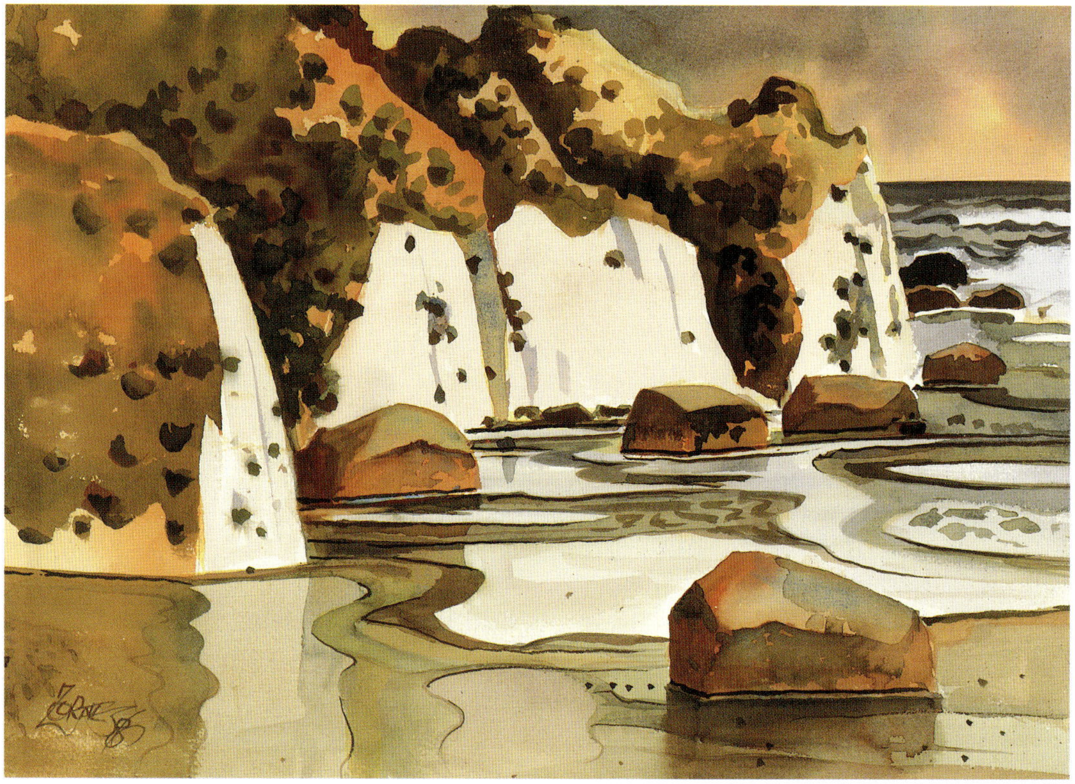

White Cliffs of Avila. 1985 Watercolor 22 x 30 in. John and Nancy Weare Collection.

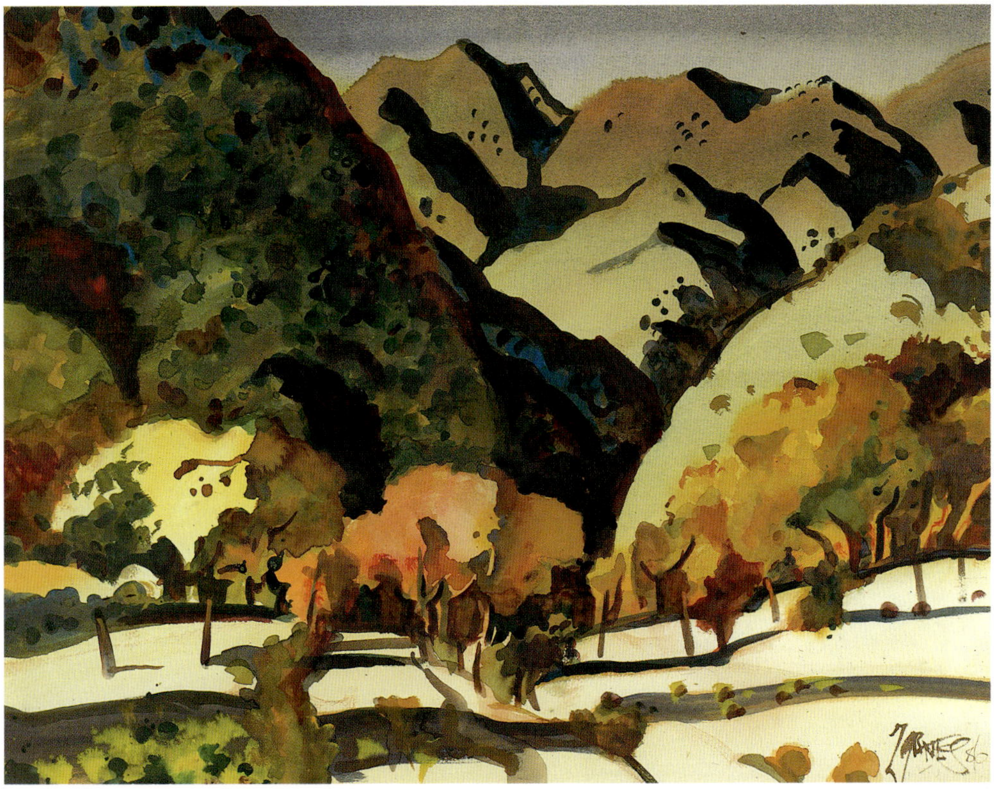

Morning Light, Cuyama. 1986 Watercolor 25 x 30 in.

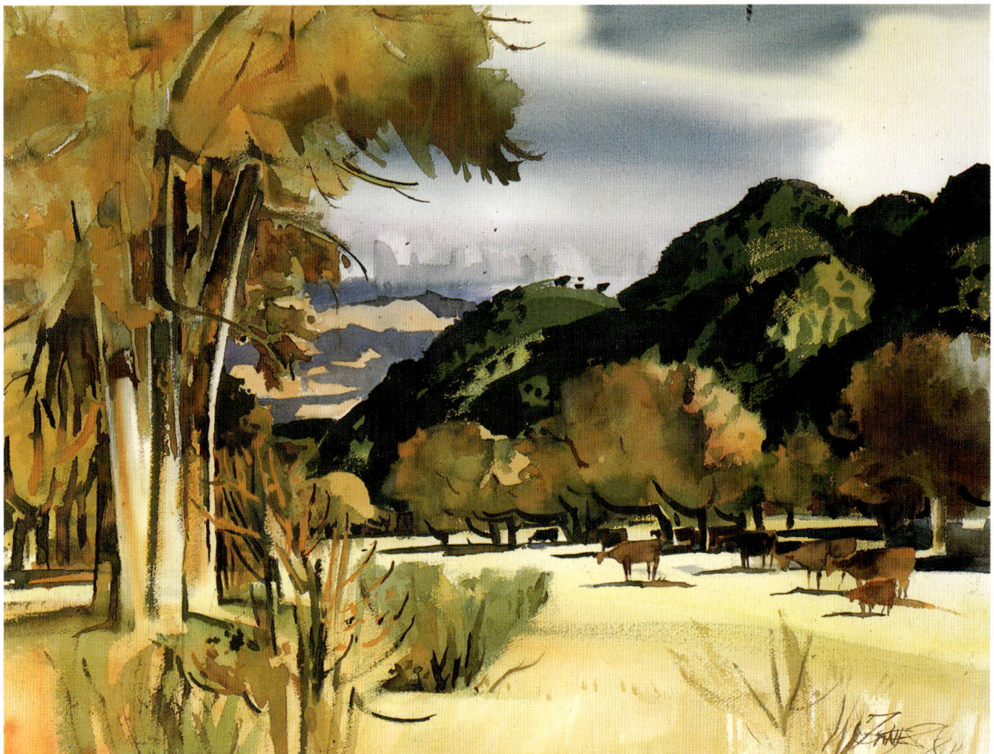

In the Cuyama. Watercolor 25 x 30 in. Corcoran Gallery of Art.

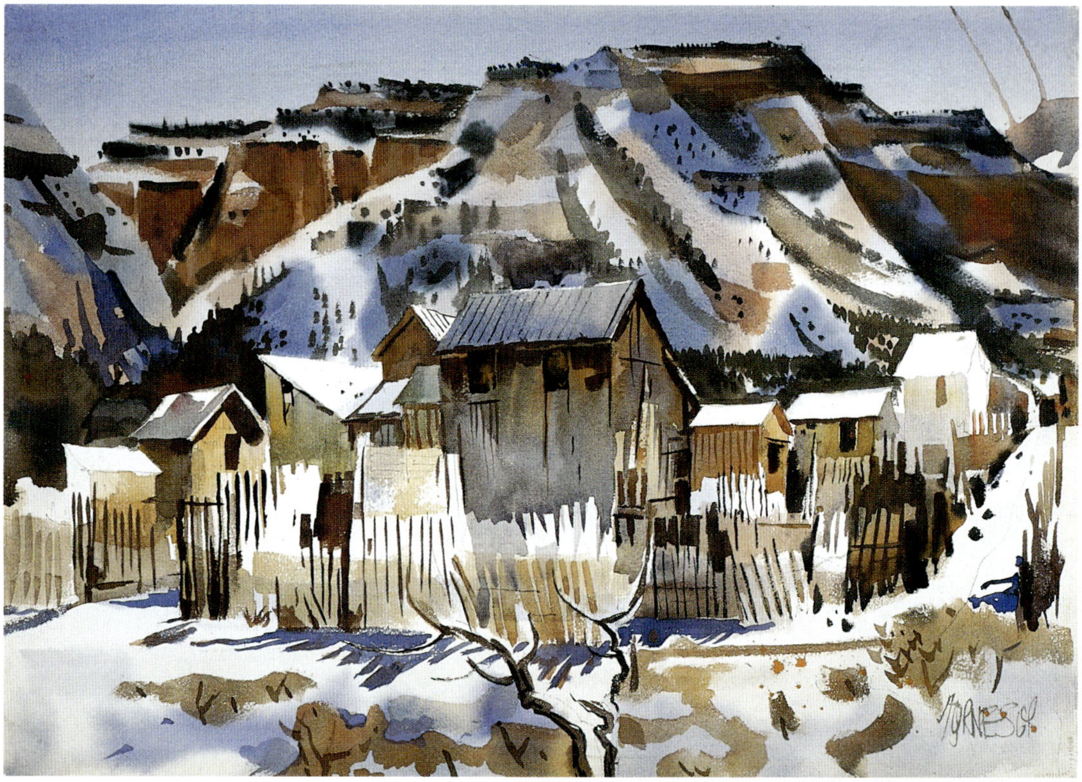

Orderville. 1979 Watercolor 22 x 30 in.

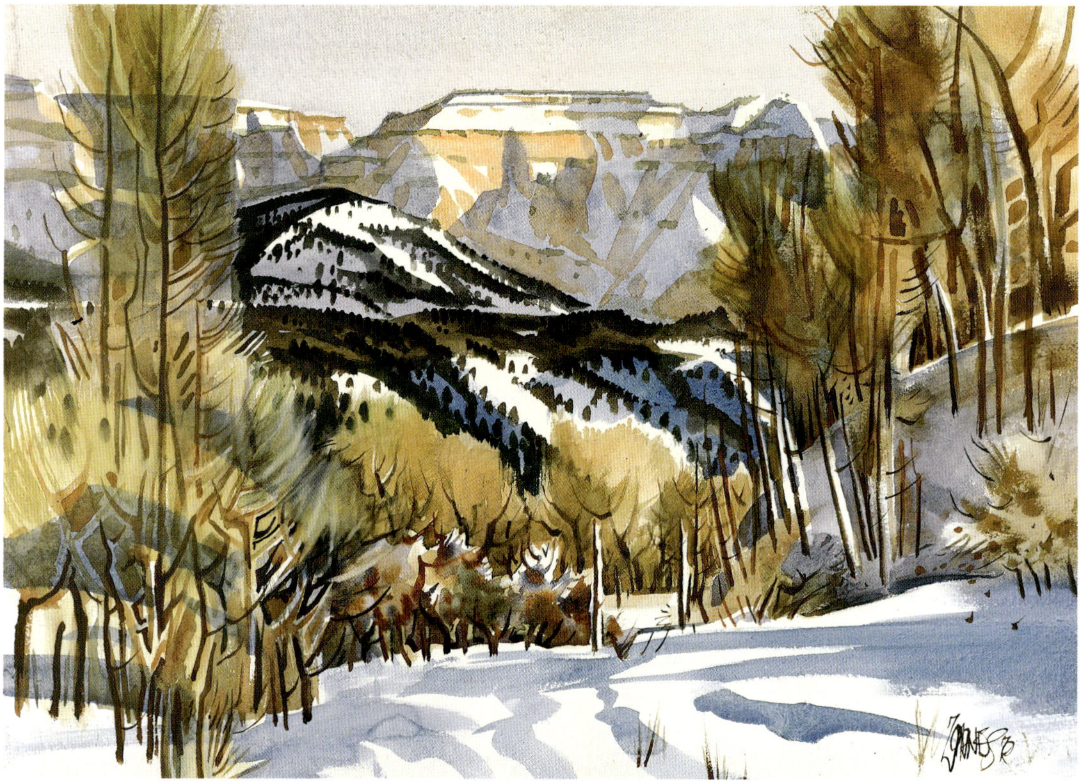

Winter at Mount Carmel 1979 Watercolor 22 x 30 in. Pat Zornes Collection

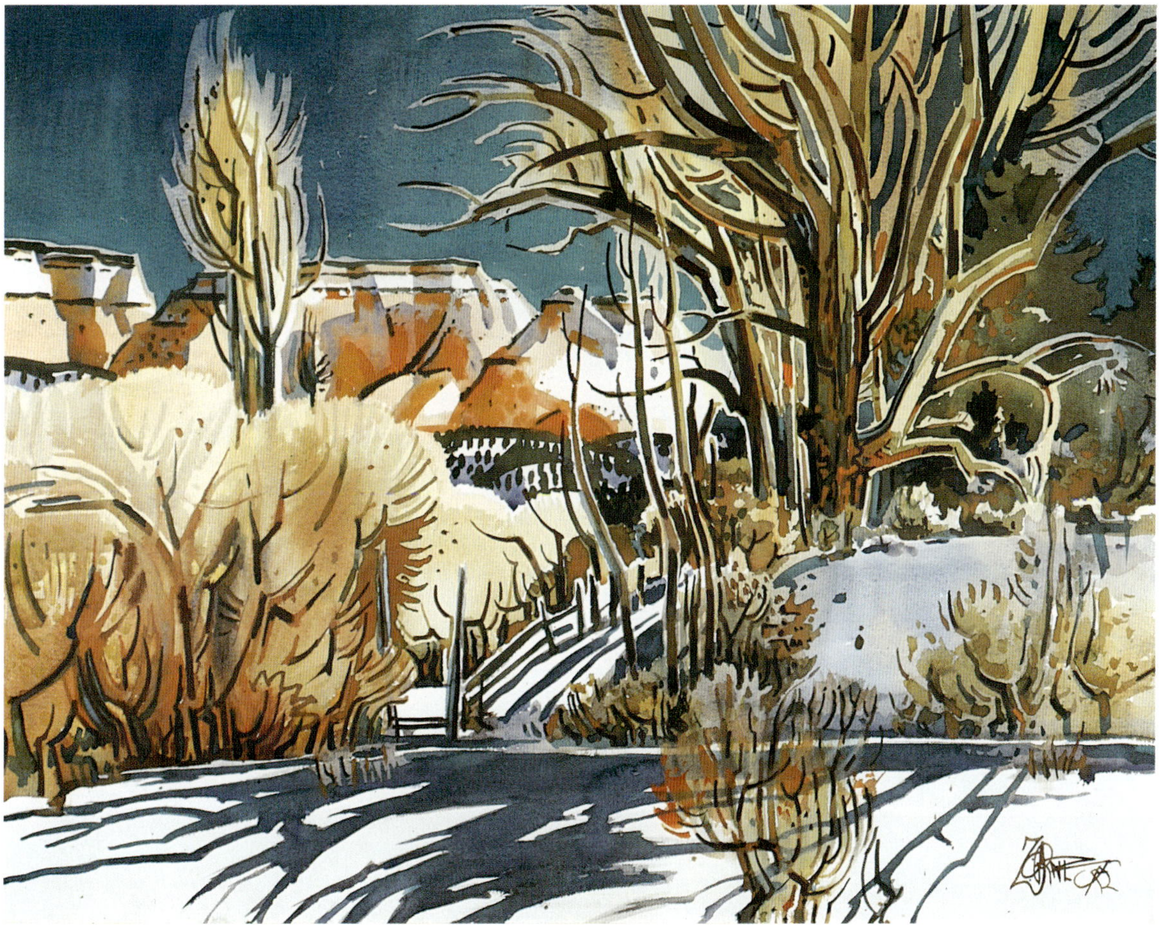

Winter in the Canyon. 1982 Watercolor 31 x 39 in. Betty Davenport Ford Collection.

is achieved by contrasting one area against another using values: warm and cool colors, complimentary colors, intense versus neutral color, hues and textures.

Once my paintings reach this stage I seek to inject additional emotion and/or drama through overstating or understating with the finishing touches. Sometimes this is done while right on location, other times I do it at a later date in my studio.''

As for Zornes' philosophy about art he states: ''I'd say I try my best to communicate through my art; art for arts sake is of little interest to me. It seems to me that if an artist produces a well composed, colored and executed work of art and maintains integrity as an individual, personal style will emerge. I also believe it to be of upmost importance that an artist is interested in living first and pursuing art as an expression of the experiences.''

Although Zornes recognizes the progress he has made through the years he continues to feel his best paintings are yet to come. This drive to create and further develop his abilities as a painter has increased his interest in

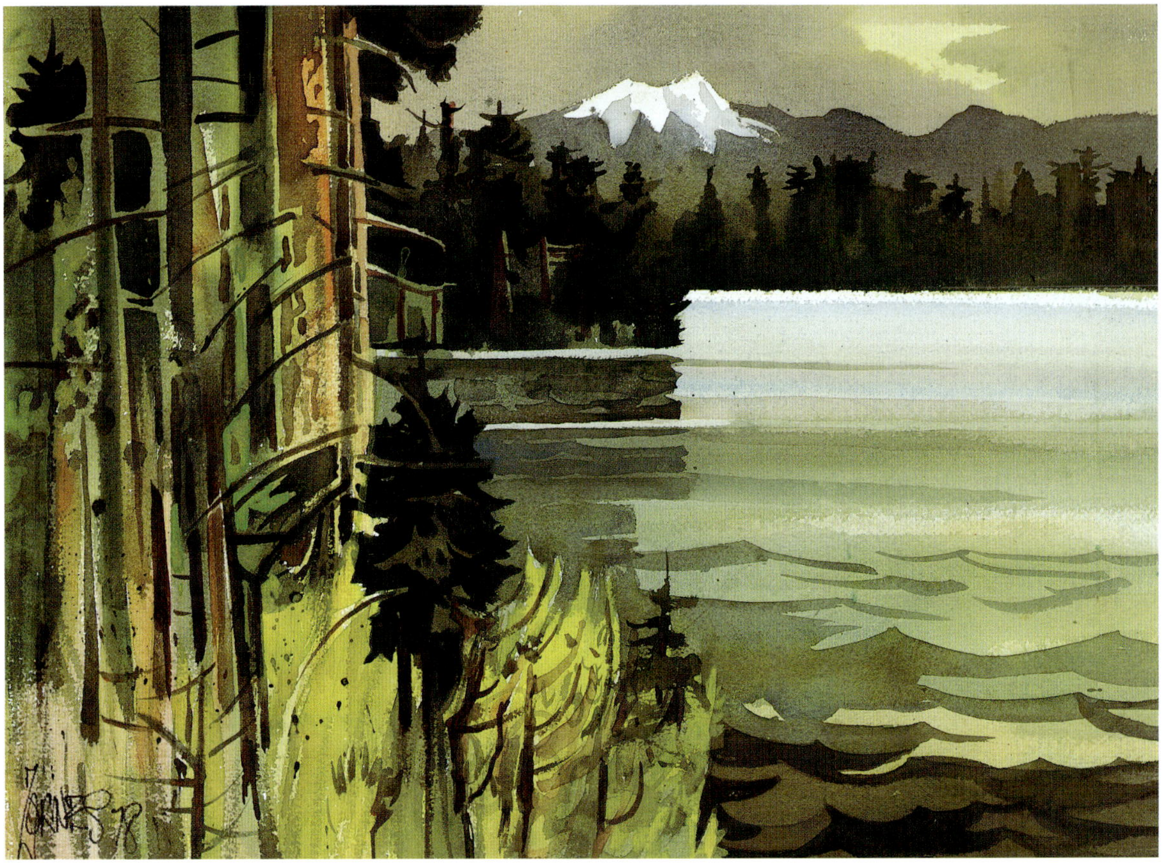

Yellowstone Lake. 1978 Watercolor 22 x 30 in.

art and helped maintain an energy level necessary to produce art on a daily basis. His works have received acclaim from his peers and the general public when put on display in one-man and group exhibitions. This has added support and given him the satisfaction of knowing his art is communicating to others in a personal way.

In an article Zornes wrote for the November 1963 issue of *American Artist* magazine he stated: "This, I believe, is what watercolor painting should be or can be—a moment in time—an immediate expression which sums up all of an artist's experience and skill and the substance of his artistic thought much as a surgeon brings all of his training to bear during an operation, or as an athlete combines the exercise of mind and body to execute a critical play."

He went on to say: "One should, I suppose, be apologetic for an art career, characterized for the most part, by the practice of many years of sitting on a hill some place trying to make a watercolor work, but my hills have been in remote and unusual places in the world from China to India to Mexico and from Hobart to Greenland; and I must believe that in long hours spent in the sun and wind, by the sea, in some mountain place or city street, I have found, and continue to find, real adventure."

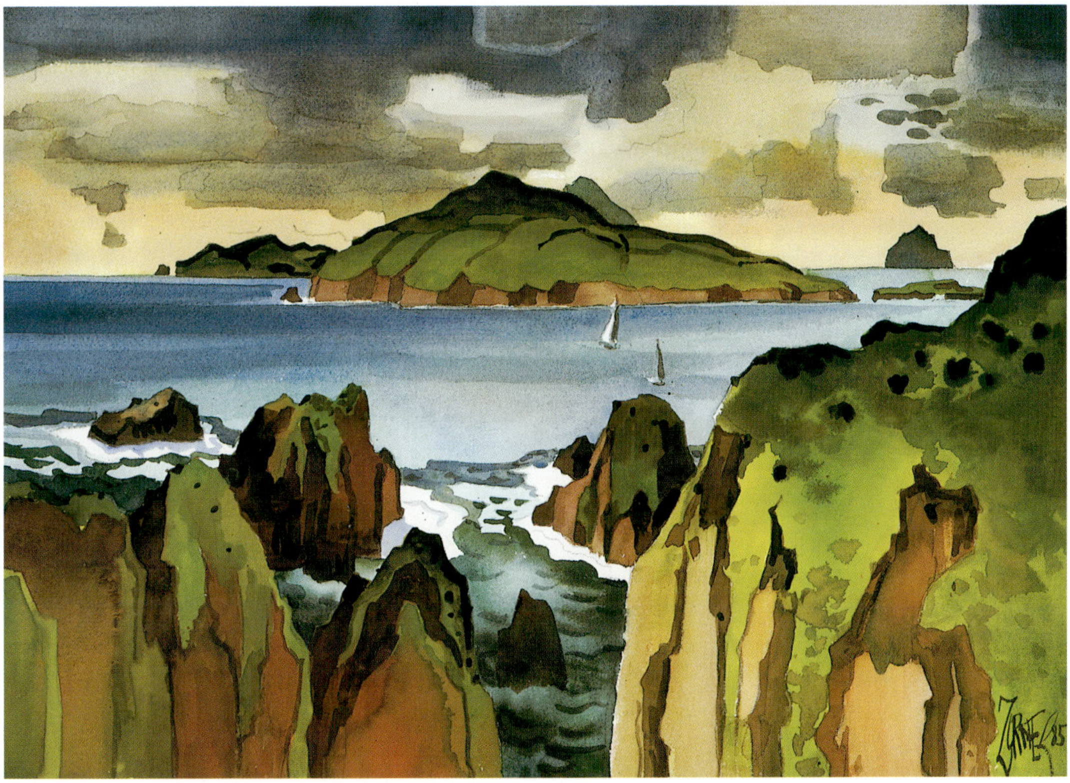

The Blasket Isles of Ireland. 1985 Watercolor 22 x 30 in. The Buck Collection.

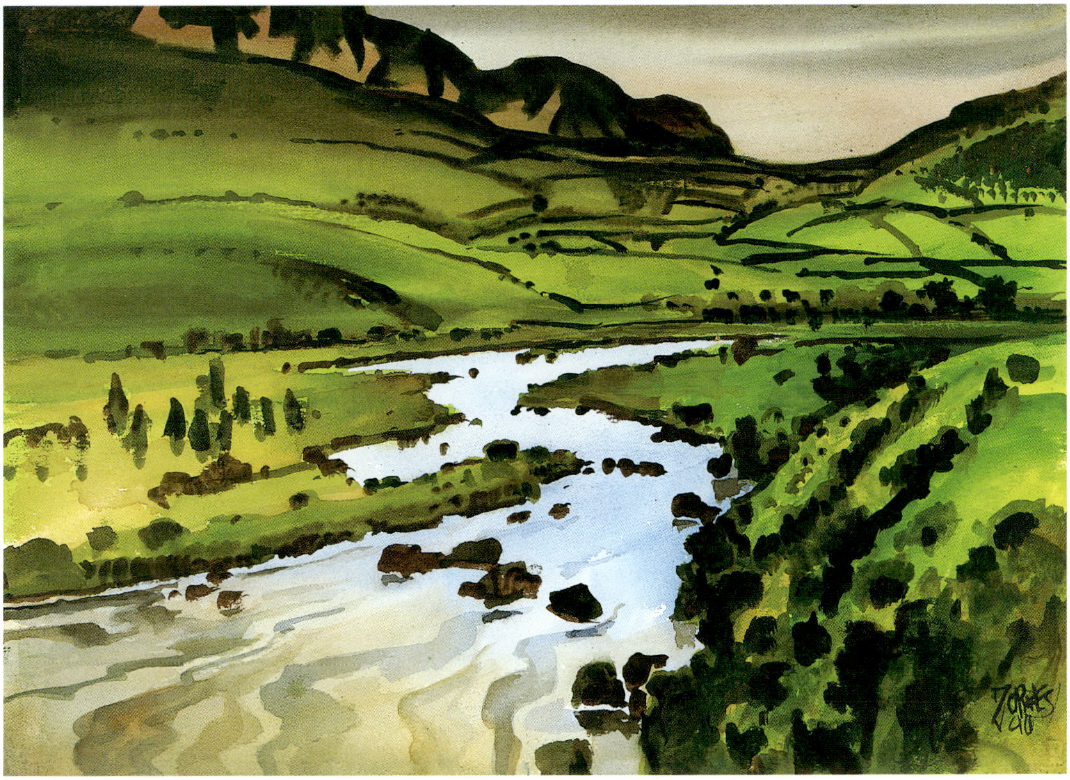

Lands of Kerry. 1990 Watercolor 22 x 30 in. The Buck Collection.

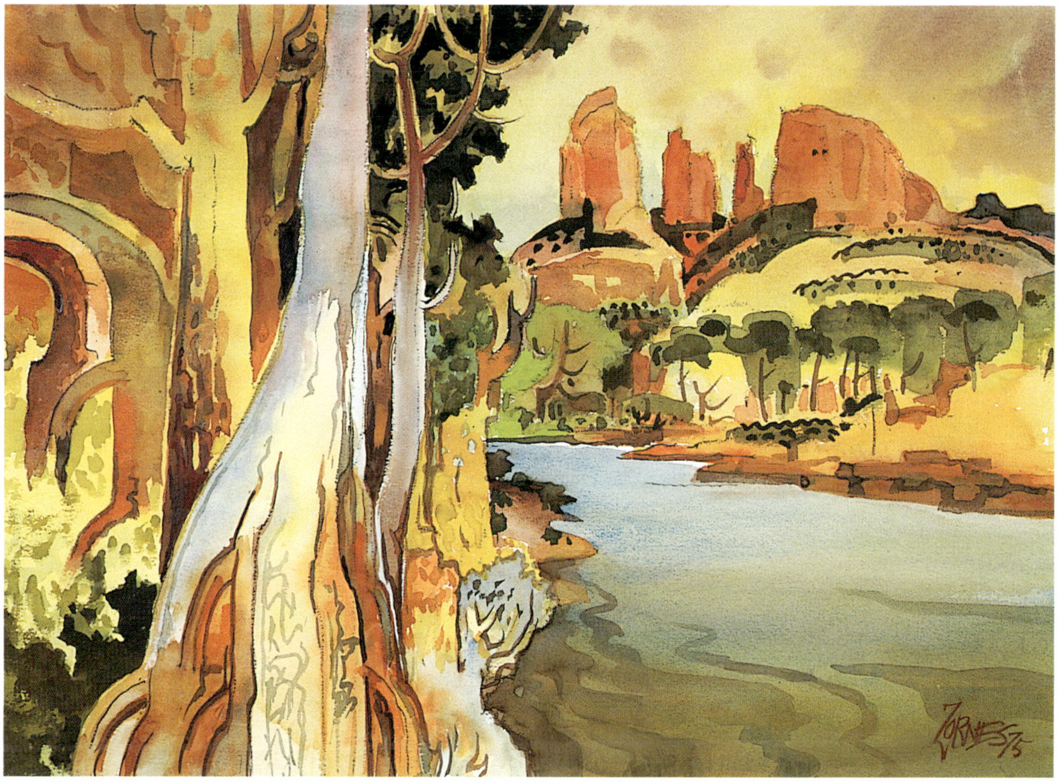

Red Rock Crossing. 1975 Watercolor 22 x 30 in.

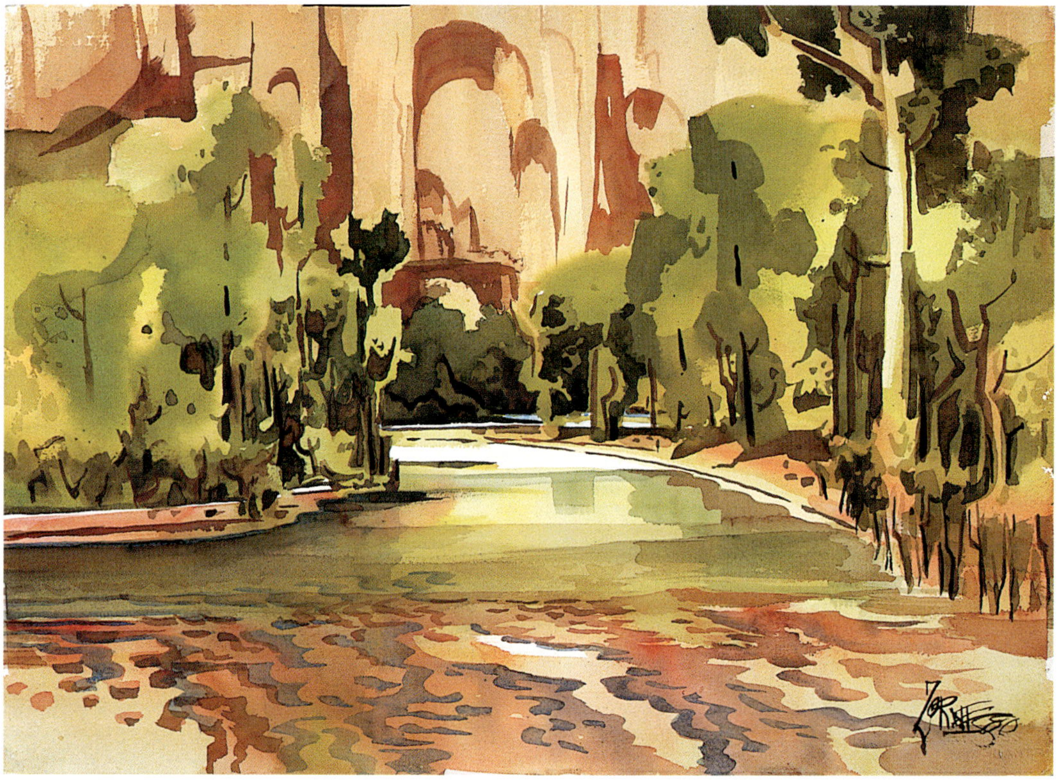

Zion Canyon. 1985 Watercolor 22 x 30 in.

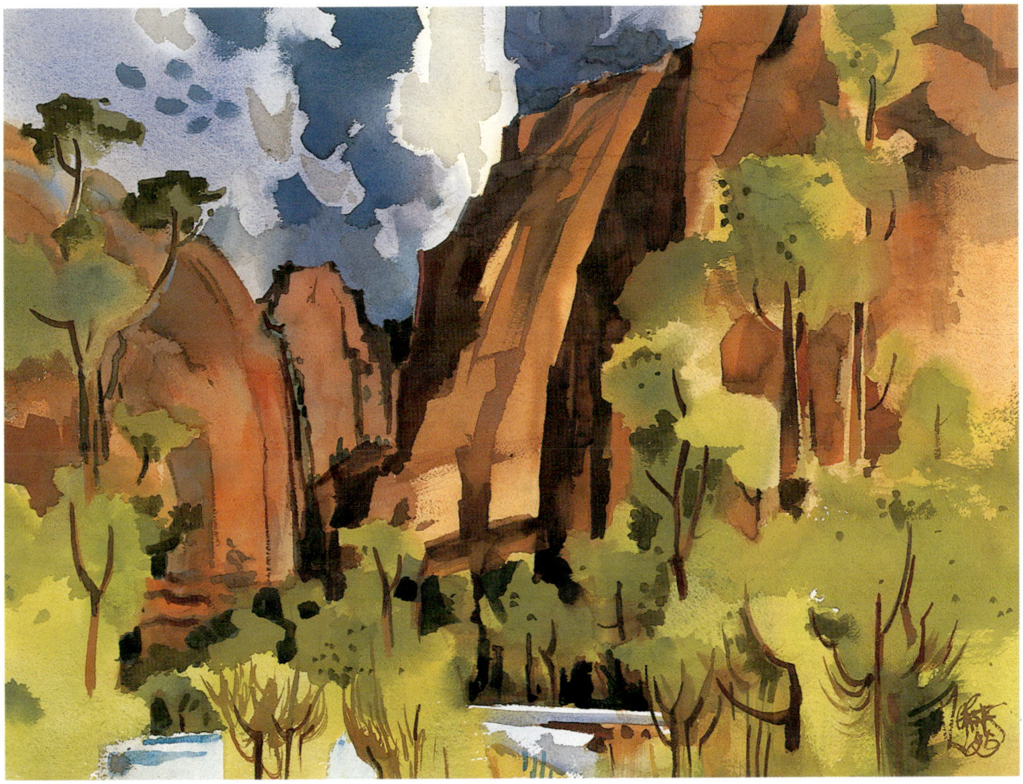

In Zion. 1985 Watercolor 22 x 30 in.

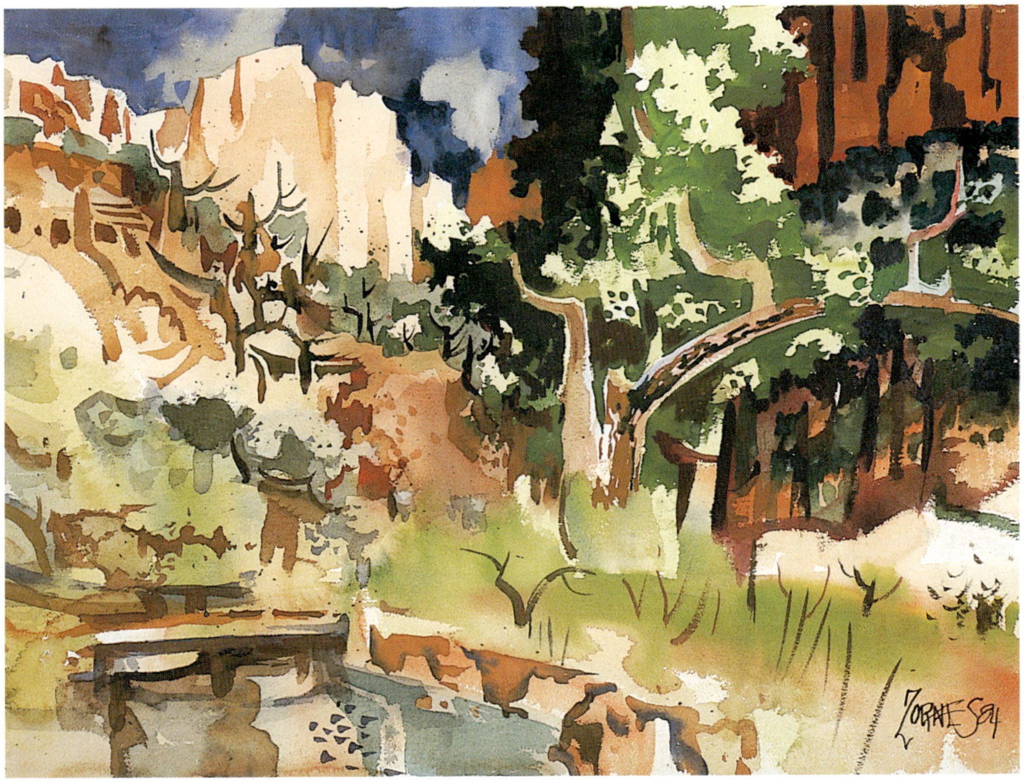

Maxwell Canyon. 1984 Watercolor 22 x 30 in. Courtesy Barbara Beretich.

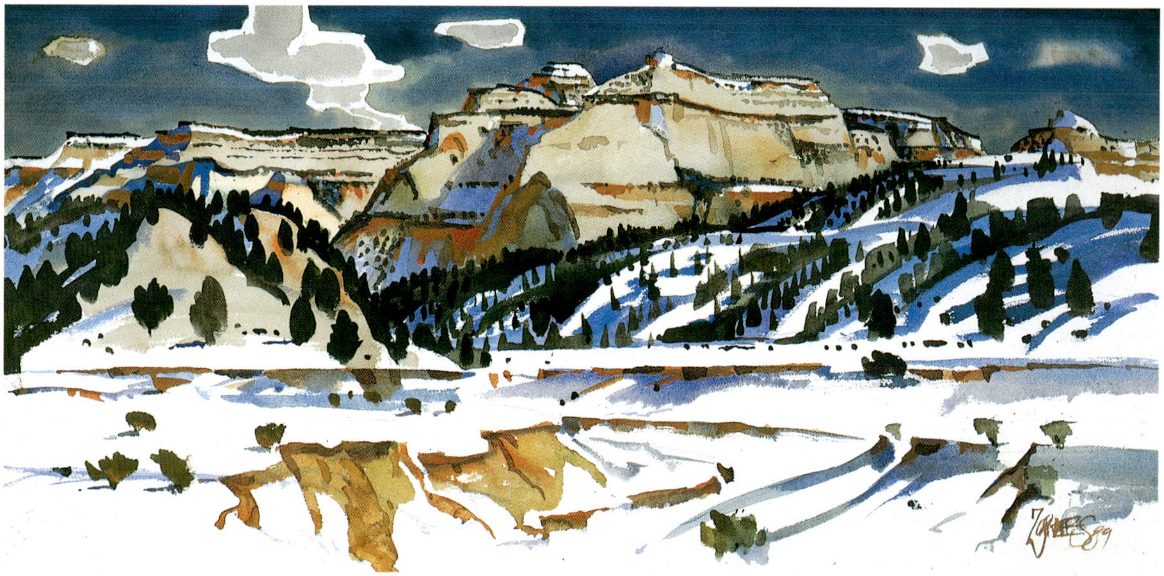

Carmel Cliffs. 1989 Watercolor 24 x 48 in.

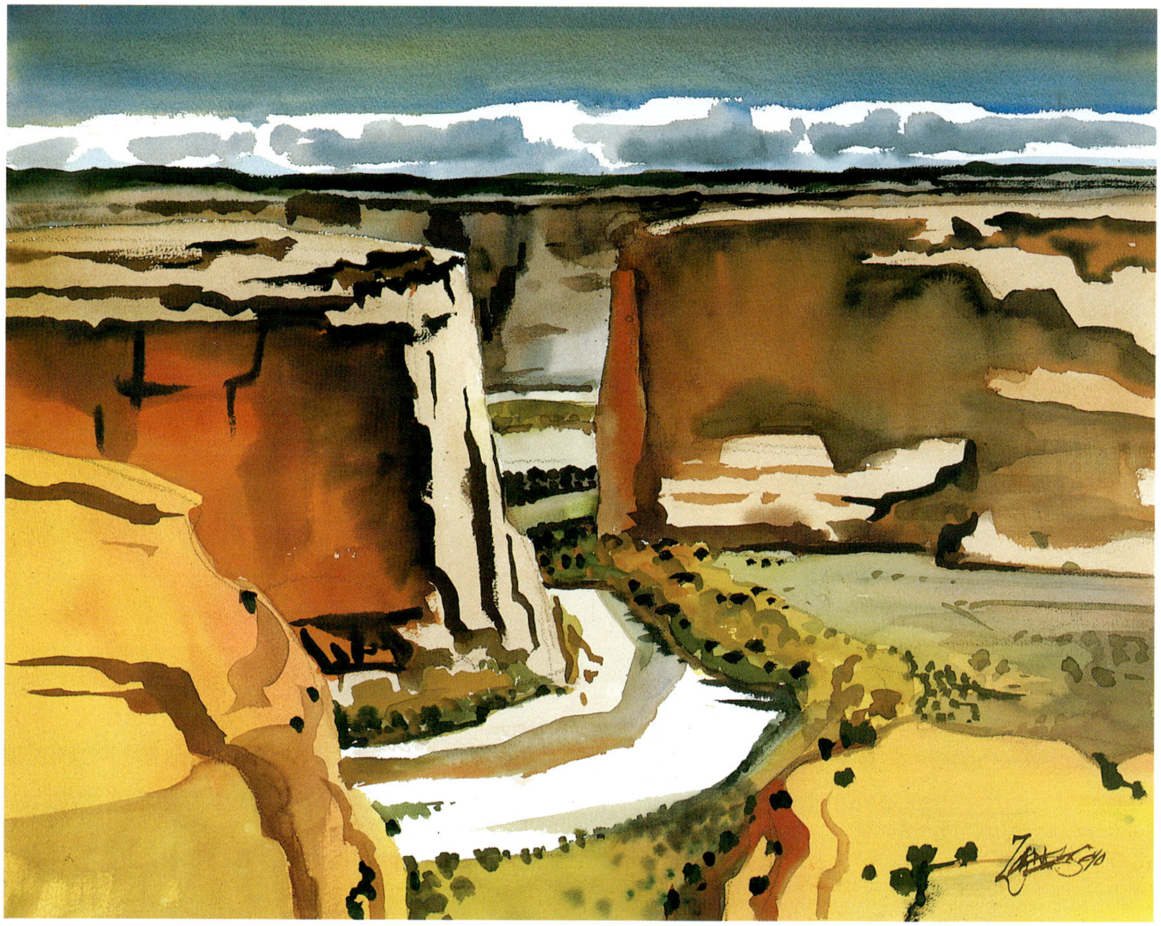

Canyon de Chelly. 1990 Watercolor 22 x 30 in. John and Barbara McFarland Collection.

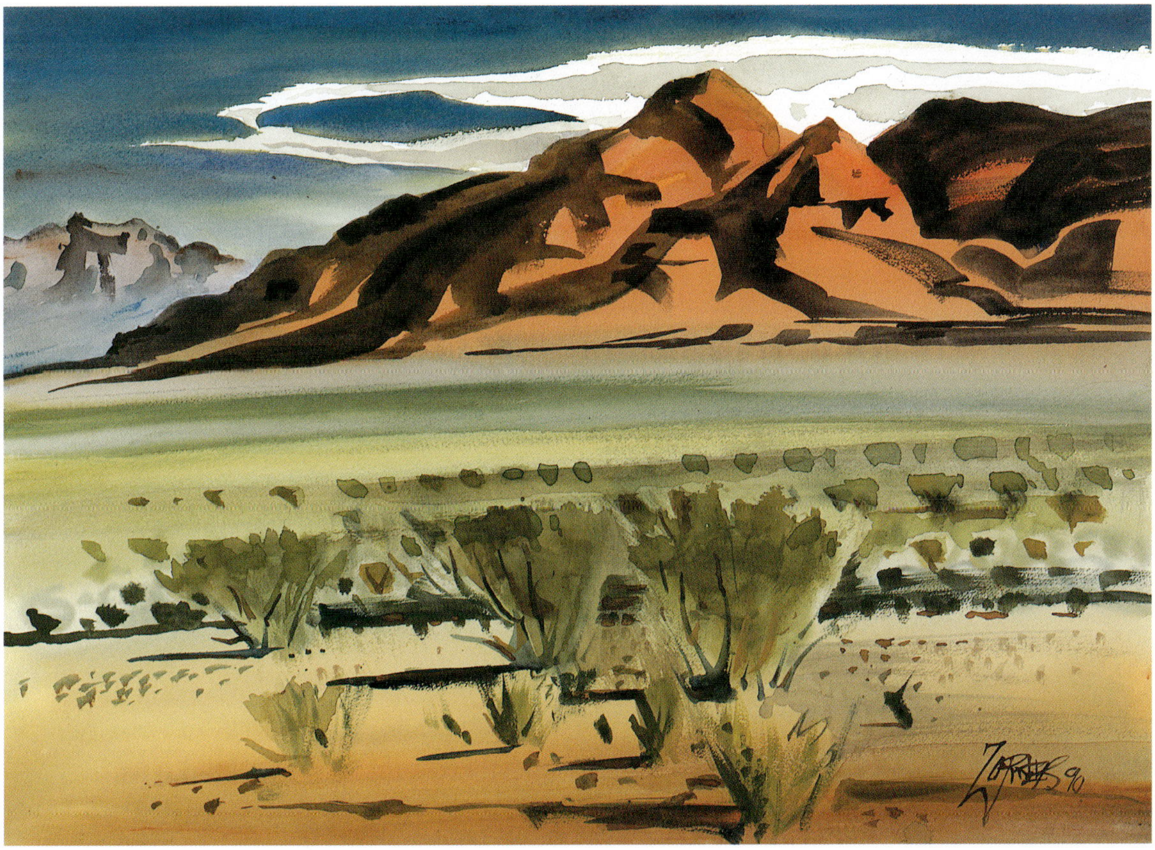

Morning on the High Desert. 1990 Watercolor 22 x 30 in.

Chronology

1908 Born James Milford Zornes on January 25, in Camargo, Oklahoma. His father James Francis was a farmer/rancher and his mother Clara a school teacher.

1911 Virginia Zornes, Milford's sister was born.

1914-1922 Milford's mother gave him basic art instruction and encouraged him to read adventure stories.

1922 Zornes family moved to Boise, Idaho.

1925 Zornes family moved to Southern California. Milford stayed in Idaho and worked for the U.S. General Land Office Survey Service as a lineman on a survey crew. In the fall he joined his family in California.

1926 Zornes graduated from San Fernando High School.

1927 Moved to Santa Maria, California and attended Santa Maria Junior College. Worked as a freelance writer.

1928 Traveled to San Francisco and studied for a brief period at Hearld's Engineering School. Hitch-hiked to San Diego, then across America to New York City.

1929 Worked on the docks in New York City while waiting to ship out as a merchant marine. Worked his way to Denmark aboard a Moore-McCormick Line freighter, then traveled across Europe, returned to New York, visited art galleries on the East Coast, then worked his way to Los Angeles via the Panama Canal on the S.S. Marian Otis Chandler.

1930 Attended the Otis Art Institute and received instruction from F. Tolles Chamberlin. Attended Glendale Junior College.

1931 Received a scholarship to study at Pomona College in Claremont, California. Studied with Millard Sheets. Awarded first place for best student painting in the annual Pomona College Art Exhibition.

1932 Continued art education at Pomona College and traveled throughout California with fellow artist Tom Craig painting depictions of regional subjects with watercolors and oils on canvas.

1933 Received a science scholarship for additional studies at Pomona College. Produced illustrations for the *Botanical Manual of Plants of Southern California* by Dr. P. A. Munz. First prize for watercolor titled *On a Beaumont Ranch* exhibited at the Los Angeles County Fair Art Exhibition.

1934 Began producing art for the P.W.A.P., a government funded art project. One-man show of watercolors at the Corcoran Gallery of Art in Washington D.C. Watercolor painting titled *Old Adobe* was selected by President and Mrs. Franklin D. Roosevelt to hang in the White House. Exhibition of Zornes watercolors at Elliot O'Hara's Watercolor Gallery, Goose Rocks Beach, Maine. Elected member of the California Water Color Society. One-man exhibit of watercolors at Scripps College, Claremont.

1935-1940 Married to Gloria Codd.

1935 Produced art for the S.E.R.A. government funded art project. Traveled across America with his wife Gloria, then together they took a pleasure cruise to England. Produced a series of watercolors depicting English landscapes and cityscapes. One-man exhibit of watercolor paintings at the Jake Zeitlin Gallery in Los Angeles. Watercolor painting titled *New Green* was exhibited at the California Pacific International Exposition in San Diego, then purchased for the collection of the Los Angeles County Museum of Art. One-man exhibit of watercolors at the Hesse Galleries, Glendale, California. One-man exhibit of watercolors at the Laguna Beach Museum of Art, California.

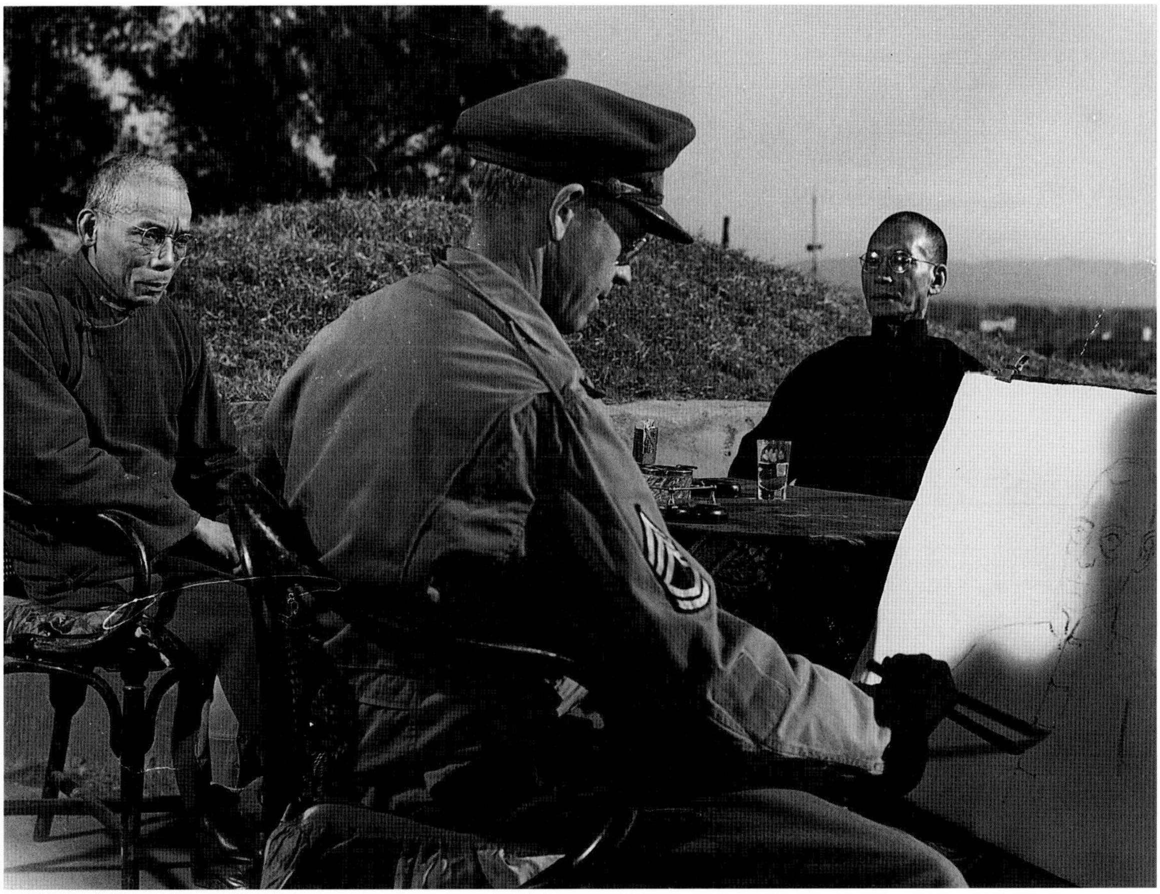

Milford Zornes at work as an official U.S. Army War Artist during World War Two. Here he is painting a portrait of Yuu Lung, the Provincial Governor of Yunnan Province and a Chinese War Lord; his secretary looks on.

1936	Painted murals for the Claremont Post Office as part of the Treasury Relief Art Project, a division of the well-known W.P.A. government funded organization. One-man exhibit of watercolors at Scripps Fine Arts Gallery, Claremont, California.
1936-1941	Worked as an art instructor at Polytechnic School in Pasadena, California.
1937	One-man exhibit of watercolors at the Butler Art Institute in Youngstown, Ohio. One-man exhibit of watercolors at the Lawrence Art Galleries in Dallas, Texas. One-man exhibit of watercolors at the Gallery of Modern Masters, Washington D.C. First prize for watercolor exhibited at the San Diego Fine Arts Gallery. Purchase prize for watercolor titled *The Coal Jetty*, exhibited in the annual show at the Butler Art Institute, Ohio. One-man exhibit of watercolors at the Wichita Art Museum, Kansas.
1938	Watercolor painting titled *Well at Guadalupe* received the William H. Tuthill award from the Art Institute of Chicago International Watercolor Exhibition. One-man exhibit of watercolors at the Walker Galleries in New York City. First prize for watercolor titled *Afternoon at Arlington*, exhibited in the annual exhibit at the San Diego Fine Arts Gallery, California. One-man exhibit of watercolors at Pomona College, Claremont, California.
1938-1942	Art instructor at the Otis Art Institute in Los Angeles.

1939 On March 28, a son, Franz Milford Zornes was born to Milford and Gloria Zornes. Traveled to Texas on a painting and sketching expedition to get ideas for a mural project. One-man exhibit of watercolors at the Pottinger Gallery in Pasadena, California. Assisted Millard Sheets in producing murals for the Golden Gate International Exposition on Treasure Island, San Francisco. Completed a mural for the United States Post Office in El Campo, Texas and returned to help install it.

1940 Watercolor titled *Arizona Evening* was purchased for the permanent collection of the Metropolitan Museum of Art in New York City. First prize for watercolor shown in the Art Institute of Chicago International Watercolor Exhibition. One-man exhibit of watercolors at the Walker Galleries in New York City. One-man exhibit of watercolors at the Jake Zeitlin Gallery in Los Angeles. One-man exhibit of watercolors, oils and drawings at Scripps Fine Arts Gallery, Claremont, California.

1941 One-man exhibit of watercolors at the Biltmore Salon, Los Angeles. One-man exhibit of watercolors at Occidental College, Los Angeles. Instructor of watercolor painting at the San Diego Fine Arts Gallery.

1941-1942 President of the California Water Color Society.

1942 Married Pat Palmer. One-man exhibit of watercolors at the Biltmore Salon, Los Angeles. Art instructor for summer sessions at Scripps College in Claremont, California. Employed by the Walt Disney Studios painting background subjects on glass plates for the animated film *Victory Through Air Power.*

1943 One-man exhibit of watercolors at the Los Angeles County Museum of Art. One-man exhibit of oil paintings and watercolors at the Stendahl Galleries in Los Angeles. One-man exhibit of drawings and watercolors at the Santa Barbara Museum of Art. One-man exhibit of watercolors at the Gump's Galleries in San Francisco.

1943-1945 Was drafted into the U.S. Army and given the assignment to record the war as an official U.S. Army War Artist. Traveled to India, Burma and China. Received first prize for watercolor exhibited in the United Nations Art Exhibit in Bombay, India.

1944 A daughter, Maria Patricia was born to Milford and Pat Zornes.

1945 After World War II Zornes resumed his teaching position at the Otis Art Institute in Los Angeles. In November he purchased a farm in Nipomo, a small town near the ocean in Central California. One-man exhibit of watercolors at Hancock College in Santa Maria, California.

1946 Traveled to Tuscon, Arizona where he and Buck Weaver helped Edith Hamlin Dixon finish two murals that Maynard Dixon started before passing away. They were later mounted on the walls of the Santa Fe ticket office in Chicago, Illinois. Hired to teach art at Pomona College in Claremont, California. Moved from Nipomo to Claremont. Received a purchase prize award from an art exhibition at Pomona College.

1947 One-man exhibit of watercolors at the Pasadena Art Institute, California.

1948 Elected a member of the American Watercolor Society. Art instructor for summer sessions at the University of California, Santa Barbara. Traveled to Alaska aboard the S.S. Alaska Cruise Line to produce a series of watercolor paintings. One-man exhibit of watercolors at Pomona College, Claremont, California, featuring works done in Alaska. One-man exhibit of oil paintings and watercolors at the Wilshire Gallery in Tuscon, Arizona.

1949 Traveled to Cripple Creek, Colorado to produce a series of watercolors depicting scenes of that region. Art instructor for summer sessions at the University of California, Santa Barbara. One-man exhibit of watercolors and drawings at the Santa Barbara Museum of Art. One-man exhibit of watercolors at the Rotunda Gallery, San Francisco. One-man exhibit of watercolors at the La Jolla Gallery of Art, California. One-man exhibit of oil paintings and watercolors at Pomona College, Claremont, California. One-man exhibit of watercolors at the David Howell Gallery, Claremont, California. One-man show of watercolors and prints at the Zeitlin and Ver Brugge Gallery, Los Angeles, California.

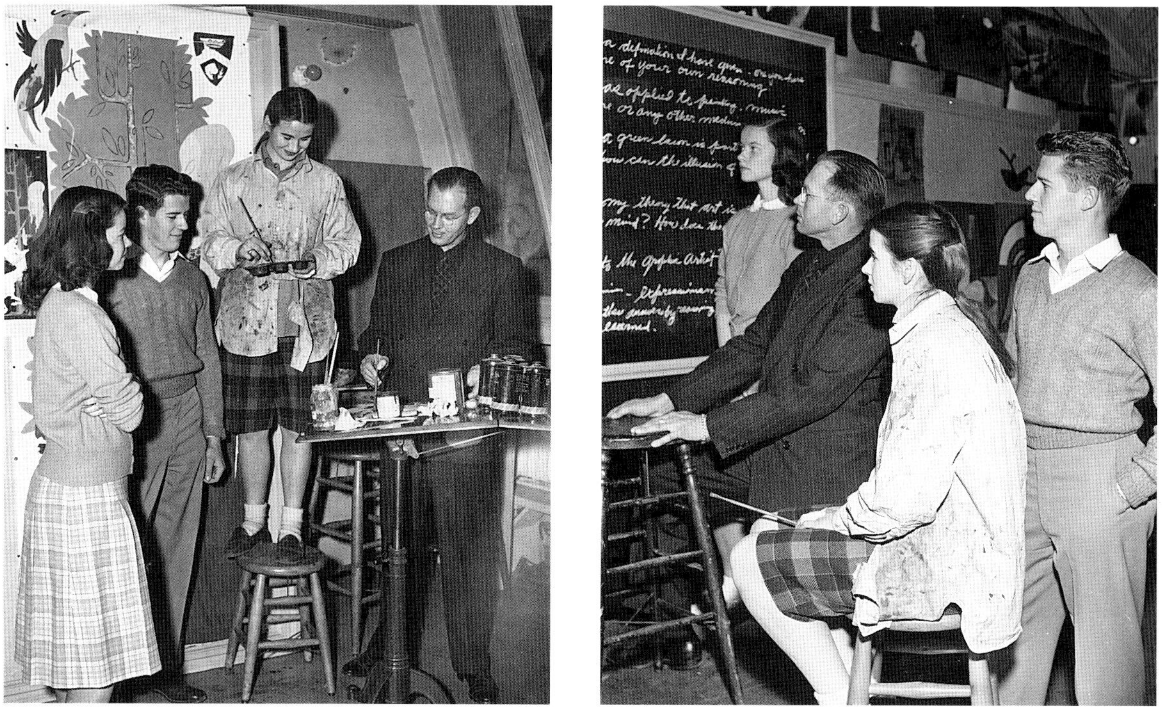

Milford Zornes and students at Pomona College, Claremont. circa. 1948.

1963 Purchased a large log cabin built by Maynard Dixon at Mt. Carmel, Utah. Received a medal of honor for a watercolor titled *Beach Party* exhibited in the American Watercolor Society Annual Exhibition in New York City. Feature article on Milford Zornes appeared in American Artist Magazine in the November issue. Purchase prize for a watercolor exhibited in the Los Angeles City Art Exhibition at the Barnsdale Park Gallery, Los Angeles. Major exhibition of watercolors by Milford Zornes, Millard Sheets, Rex Brandt and Peter Hurd held at the Southwest Art Gallery in Palm Desert, California. One-man exhibit of watercolors at the White Gallery in Montrose, California. Painting excursion to Spain and the island of Majorca. Held Milford Zornes Landscape Class in watercolor painting at Laguna Beach.

1963-1976 Formed the Zornes Watercolor Workshop to teach watercolor painting at his studio in Mt. Carmel, Utah.

1964 Elected an Associate of the National Academy of Design (A.N.A.). One-man exhibit of watercolors at Chaffey College Art Gallery in Alta Loma, California. One-man exhibit of watercolors at the Steppan Gallery in San Bernardino, California. One-man exhibit of watercolors at the White Gallery in Montrose, California. Two-man exhibit of watercolors with Rex Brandt at the Southwest Art Gallery in Palm Desert, California.

1965 Held Zornes Watercolor Workshop classes in Newport Beach and Laguna Beach, California. One-man exhibit of watercolors at the Cunningham Museum in Bakersfield, California. One-man exhibit of watercolors at the Fine Arts Gallery in Riverside, California. One-man exhibit of watercolors at the Steppan Galleries in San Bernardino, California. One-man exhibit of watercolors at the White Gallery in Montrose, California. Two-man exhibit of watercolors with Phil Dike at the Dorian Hunter Gallery in Fullerton, California.